p.s.

WHAT I DIDN'T SAY

Unsent Letters to Our Female Friends

Edited by Megan McMorris

SEAL PRESS

P.S.
What I Didn't Say
Copyright © 2009 Megan McMorris

Published by Seal Press
A member of the Perseus Books Group
1700 Fourth Street
Berkeley, CA 94710

Library of Congress Cataloging-in-Publication Data

P.S. : what I didn't say / edited by Megan McMorris.
    p. cm.
Includes bibliographical references and index.
ISBN 978-1-58005-290-0 (alk. paper)
1. Female friendship. 2. Interpersonal communication. 3.
Women--Correspondence. I. McMorris, Megan.
HQ1206.P195 2009
302.3'4082--dc22
                        2009011929

Cover design by Gerilyn Attebery
Interior design by Tabitha Lahr
Printed in the United States of America
Distributed by Publishers Group West

To my childhood McBuddies—
Andy (Mc)Shemberg, Diane McEwen-Martin,
and Heather McCracken—for continuing to show this
girl true friendship thirtysome years later.

You rock, dudes.

contents

note from the editor: bffs, frenemies, and everything in between

Yesterday, I was having one of those days. You know, when you're rushing around from the time you wake up until suddenly it's 6:00 and you have more work to finish, but you have to hop in the shower and go out to meet a friend.

It was my own fault. It was a bad idea to have booked tickets for the musical *Wicked* (to celebrate my friend Anne Marie's birthday the previous month) three days before my deadline for this very book you hold in your hands. But I've never been a good planner-aheader. You see, I'm typically quite laid-back about a big deadline until, oh, two weeks before, upon which time I morph into a sweet-Jesus-how-am-I-going-to-get-this-done-forgot-to-eat-or-shower-today-except-where-are-those-Twizzlers-and-honey-can-you-pick-up-some-Pepsi-Max-and-a-bottle-of-red-wine-when-you-get-home types.

x PS: what i didn't say

That night, I wanted nothing more than to get into my pj's, finish editing that essay I was working on, and watch a couple episodes of *The Real Housewives of Atlanta* (last I'd left off, things had just started to heat up between NeNe and Kim!).

Instead, I forced myself into the shower, rummaged through my overflowing pile of laundry to find some clean clothes, and made it to the theater just in time. As soon as I saw Anne Marie, though, I was glad to be out among the living. She marveled at the fact that I had managed to dress up and wanted to hear everything about the book, and I felt myself relaxing as I told her my progress.

After a brief moment at the theater's ATM (which Anne Marie managed to turn into a comedy routine, comparing it to a slot machine as a long line formed behind her; you had to be there, but I was in tears), she stopped me in front of the wine bar.

"Okay, missy, let's get you a glass of wine—since you got the tickets, it's my treat!" Once we got to the front of the line, she nudged me. "Psst . . . Meg, why don't you get two?" (This from a woman who has been sober for seven years. Now, *that's* what you call a true friend!)

We stood among the pre-theater crowd, me double-fisting wine, her sipping soda, and I told her about some of my favorite stories in this book. By the time we took our seats for the fitting friendship story of *Wicked,* I was happy to be away from my computer and out of the house altogether. But most of all, I was feeling grateful to have a friend like Anne Marie, whom I've known for twenty years—since our freshman year at Indiana U.—and who knows me better than most anyone. When I'm most stressed, she can always find a way to make me laugh,

and she never judges me if, as a matter of fact, I *do* wan
second glass of wine, thanks for asking!

That's the thing about putting together a friendship anthology—you end up analyzing, appreciating, and acknowledging your own friends. The fact that this book's timing coincided with the Facebook explosion made things even more interesting. Suddenly, I was reconnecting with plenty of old friends, including The One That Got Away. The one I'd always wondered about. And rather than finally getting an answer for why she had disappeared on all of us after graduating a semester early from high school (even though she had made me promise that we were going to remain friends, even though we had been great buddies since second grade) I got a glossed-over message about how she was happy to be in touch, how she was impressed with all of my writing accomplishments, and how she wanted to keep in touch more. It hasn't happened. It wasn't enough. But at least I finally had closure on a fallen friendship.

I'm the first to admit I'm a sentimental soul when it comes to those who have passed through, or who have become big players in my life. And that's part of the reason I came up with this book idea. To celebrate, to examine, and to be brutally honest about friendship. And I realized that I wasn't alone: Asking contributors to participate made me realize that we all have some kind of friendship story that is worth writing home about.

When I was reading the submissions, it was easy for me to see myself in them. In "An Ode to My Partner in Crime," Bevin Wallace's hysterical antics with her childhood best friend (which included winning an air-band competition with the song *Let's Do the Time Warp Again*) made me laugh out loud, reminding me of my best childhood pal, Andy, and myself in matching uniforms and top hats and canes, dancing to the song *One* from *A Chorus Line* in our sixth-grade talent show (don't laugh, we came in second place—blast that adorable Adam McElwain, with his banjo version of *Over the Rainbow*!). Other letters, like Michelle Goodman's "Fireflies," had such vivid details (feather earrings, Jordache jeans, and parachute pants, anyone?) that I felt I was back in my purple Esprit sweatshirt and jelly shoes again, feathering my hair to get ready for my ninth-grade school day to begin.

Some letters in this book show how the deepest friendships can be forged in unusual circumstances. Anna Cox examines in her shriek-with-laughter letter, "Not Sometimes, but *Always,*" how a "bad news" friend is the only kind to have when you're down (which reminded me very much of my dear friend and contributor Robin Troy, without whom I feel like I would barely have survived the year 2000). Jenna Schnuer says goodbye to her travel partner in crime, whom she immediately bonded with on the road, in "Butt Paste, Bass, and Beyond: An On-the-Road Friendship." In her shout out to all of her adventurous buddies, "The Mother of All Adventures," Katie Arnold decides that when it comes to the greatest friends, sometimes you just can't narrow it down to one. In her hysterical "Air Mail," Dimity McDowell explains how, when you're dealing with a cliquey middle school, the best of friends are those you invent. And in "Two Generations of Non-Girly Girls," Robin Troy eloquently shows us that bridging a fifty-year age gap is easy when you meet someone like her friend Evaun.

There are the darker sides too. In "Collateral Damage," Jane Hodges shows us that sometimes you just need to move on from an unbalanced friendship. (Let's just say I could relate to that one!) There's sickness—Alice Lesch Kelly gives a heartfelt salute to her fellow cancer survivor friend in "Who Needs Pink Ribbons with a Friend Like You?" There's injury—in the evocative "A Voice from the Future," Gabrielle Studenmund writes a letter to herself seven years ago, before she had a traumatic bike accident. And there's also death—in "Twenty Years Later," Judy Sutton Taylor fills her friend in on what she's missed since she was killed in the Lockerbie bombing of 1988.

But there's also deep silliness, as comedian Sara Benincasa gives a shout-out to her "buddy," Sarah Palin—whom she portrayed in an award-winning series of vlogs on the Huffington Post's humor site, 23/6—in "I'm Not You, but I Play You on the Internet: A Letter to Sarah Palin."

Then there is Jacquelyn Mitchard. Every time I read her letter, "The We of Me," my reactions come on slowly—the tightening of the throat, the short breaths, until before I know it, I'm openly sobbing, much to the consternation and wrinkled brow of my officemate, my yellow lab Luey (my other officemate, my brown tabby Lily, doesn't seem to notice). I go through each submission five times while editing, and for Jacquelyn's, I'm five for five in the dewey-eyed department. Please run, don't walk, to page 1 to discover why I can't even say "Jackie was popular, and I was the little caboose" without breaking into tears (oh great, here come the waterworks, thanks a mill!). But seriously: I'm honored that the woman who was awarded Oprah's first Book Club pick for *The Deep End of the Ocean* (which was made into a movie starring Michelle Pfeiffer) contributed to this book.

So there you have it—sickness and health, older and younger, through thick and thin—it all kinda sounds like vows in a way, doesn't it? While reading these essays, I couldn't help but think that sometimes our female friendships are like romances in the way that they affect us long after the final curtain call. From theme songs (Led Zeppelin and Ani DiFranco both seem to be on heavy rotation throughout the book) to signature drinks (Boone's Farm wine ring a bell, anyone?) to even having that daydream about running into The One That Got Away (as Sophia Dembling so perfectly describes in "A Crime against Friendship"), it's clear that we're surrounded by reminders or thoughts of our long-lost pals.

The thirty-six letters here are laugh-out-loud funny, sob-your-eyes-out sad, and show the good, the bad, and the ugly of most every kind of friendship out there, from BFFs to frenemies. I hope the letters within ring a bell with you and make you think about the great friends in your life.

But most of all, I hope that you have at least one friend like Anne Marie—one who lets you be you, who always makes you laugh, and who fully recognizes that sometimes it's perfectly fine (encouraged, even!) to double-fist wine.

Thanks for reading!

Megan McMorris

March 2009

the we of me

BY JACQUELYN MITCHARD

ear Jeanine,

If you have that one friend, you are rich.

That one friend is different from all the others, dear as they are.

There are close friends and best friends and situational friends. Their faces flash into vivid prominence for a time and then fade—as we make our way from high school and college to the first job, from the company softball team to visiting the park with our newborns, from the junior soccer league to the neighborhood dinner club and the knitting circle. Some friendships endure only through the splendid memories they bequeath. Some revive with a yearly session of intense catching up.

But some friendships, like ours, are what you once referred to, quoting Carson McCullers, as "the we of me."

There is nothing you don't know about me, nothing I don't know about you. And some of these are things neither of us will ever share with anyone else on earth—even our children, even the people we love most. When we say someone is "like us," we don't mean they grew up in the Midwest. We mean "us," an indefinable unit, a sorority of two.

When we were 13, and then 16 and even 19, there was scarcely a single weekend night we didn't spend together. College didn't intervene. Your unplanned and early motherhood didn't intervene.

But something did intervene—a sad and unintended misunderstanding.

It would be easy to say that we endured through thick and thin, good times and bad, loves and loss, the fleeting and oversold pleasures of youth, the blessings and unrelenting demands of motherhood, the excruciating and exhilarating demands of career. But it wasn't like that. For five long, bleak years, we didn't speak. For five years, we noticed in miserable silence as the other's birthday slipped past on the calendar. Neither of us even tried to plaster over the great, unsightly hole the loss left behind. Our friendship was complicated and had to heal around that breach. Perhaps because it did, and because of what came afterward, it remains one of the most treasured bonds of our lives.

It took tragedy to reunite us—and, eerily, we reunited in the nick of time.

We met more than 35 years ago, when I was 13 years old. Though I'm painfully shy, despite the ability to crack jokes easily in front of a crowd of 5,000 for a benefit speech, I'd signed up for Student Council because I thought it might save me from spending the next four years wandering the halls of a huge, urban Chicago high school utterly and shamefully alone. It was the first day of school. I'd already lost my brand-new green trench coat because the school was so big that I couldn't remember which building my locker was in. Standing there in the office, I felt ridiculous. I was trying to reduce myself to a colloid that would seep into the paneling and disappear.

I heard a voice, and because you were, and are, so small, at first I didn't even know its origin.

You asked, "Do you have a lot of friends?"

When I saw you—small, delicate, with the most beautiful eyelashes I'd ever seen—I smiled and answered, "Are you kidding? I'm the girl nobody knows."

"Well, I'm nobody," you said.

A few years after, I was an officer of the Student Council, and made school history by becoming the only girl to ever "make" the elite pom-pom squad and give it up voluntarily a day later to remain an editor on the school newspaper; I had boyfriends by the handful and friends by the score. You? You remained quiet, on the sidelines. You were like the angel in my pocket. I never excluded you. I never forsook you. Other friends sometimes wondered at our steadfast devotion, because we seemed to be such opposites.

But we weren't.

Both of us were daughters who didn't get the love we deserved.

For you, it was because your mother—who now dotes on you—was shocked to have a child ten years after the ones she'd planned. My parents had other fish to fry than spending time with a child; and the fish swam at the bottom of a highball glass. I don't think my mother or father ever attended a school event (although my mother made sure I dressed well for them—she did want me to be the prettiest *and* the thinnest girl).

Still, you and I needed so little beyond each other.

Boys came and went; we wept and drowned our sorrows in Campbell's tomato soup. In my mother's old Chevy, we cruised the west side. We ran a stick down the fence at the monastery, making such a racket that the monks let out the Dobermans while we screamed and scattered gravel pulling away. On Halloween night, we sat on Al Capone's grave, and, on a dare, drank a shot of whiskey from a flask provided by our friend Charley. I'm surprised that Mr. Capone hasn't sunk deeper than six feet under because of the weight of kids at Mount Carmel Cemetery who have tried to raise his ghost. We perched on the hood of the car at Pepe's Tacos and tried to look sophisticated smoking Salems—although neither of us could learn to inhale and we had to run into the alley to throw up. When we went to parties, we stopped first at the department store to flit from the mascara counter to the perfume aisle, because neither of us had the money for fancy makeup. We lay on a blanket on the roof porch at my parents' apartment and talked about our dreams: I was going to write great novels; you, with your lyrical, powerful voice, were going to be a Broadway star. We were good feminists. We would make it on our own, and make it big.

"I'm going to write a book by the time I'm twenty-five," I told you.

"Why one?" you pressed me. "Why not two? Why not five?"

And off we went to the state college; but you didn't stay long.

When we were freshmen, you met the boy who made you fall on your knees. He was beautiful; he was comic and talented and utterly heartless. When you learned you were pregnant, Mike pulled a disappearing act worthy of David Copperfield. You went home—to my mother, who gave you comfort and lemon ice, knitted baby blankets, took you to the movies, stayed beside you almost daily until my godchild, Gemma, was born. I loved my mother fiercely, then, and was never prouder of her. She could have been disapproving, as your own parents were. But instead, she encompassed you with her love.

But as much as she adored playing "grandma," and couldn't wait to be one in real life, Mama didn't realize that dream.

Diagnosed with a virulent brain cancer and given just months to live, she smiled, happy and bemused, as I married a boy who was just a pal—a kind of spoof so that my mom could see me in a wedding gown. You were in on the farce, as my bridesmaid. I promised forever, but let forever be quietly annulled months later. But I didn't see myself as evil to have done it. Then, I came home for good. I finished school early and worked as a waitress, to help guide my younger brother through high school. You and I were together again, with a baby seat in the back of the old car, cruising the mile-square route with The Beach Boys blasting on the radio.

But when I moved to Wisconsin to take a coveted job on a daily newspaper, it meant days of starting work at 5:00 AM on the copy desk.

Spent and challenged, I didn't get home often enough to see you through the terror you felt when your beloved father, too, learned he had cancer. No one expected that he would die so quickly. But I was too new at my job to take days off for a funeral not in my immediate family—at least, not by blood.

And so, the last words you said to me, for five years, were, "You betrayed me."

Now I said thousands of words—through the crack in the door at your apartment, in letters, in cards, pleading with you to understand.

You were stubborn. You would not.

When I married for real, you were not there. When my beloved firstborn came, you were not there to be his godmother. When my second and third sons were born, when I struggled with infertility and did indeed write my first book—on that subject—you were not there.

But when cancer came to my door, again, to claim my husband, you came, unbidden. It was years before we ever talked about the time we spent apart. All I recall is that, in the midst of a furious hell of grief, I was staggered by gratitude. If you were there, I could live through this. A dozen other friends had given me comfort and aid; but only you remembered me, for me. You held me with all the strength in your five-foot-nothing, ninety-pound frame, and I was home.

I would never let you go again.

Our weekly marathons on the telephone resumed. We dissected jobs, life, your dates, my lack of them. When others called me foolish, you told me to go ahead, to write my first novel during the two years after Dan died instead of taking "a real job." All I wanted was to finish it—to show my sons that no matter the size of the hole life drove through you, it didn't give you permission to live small. My book came through; in fact, it went over the left-field wall, chosen the first novel for Oprah Winfrey's Book Club. You cheered, as you did two years later, when I married my husband, Chris. You and I went together to California to see the filming of the movie made from my novel, *The Deep End of the Ocean*.

And at last, you graduated, with a degree in theater, and became a sought-after voice and acting teacher, winning roles on stage and in commercials. When my third son, Marty, began to sing and act, you coached him with the same unsparing honesty and compassion you gave me when you read my pages.

You weren't yet forty when your legs began to hurt.

Deep into my aerobics period, I teased you. "It's because you're such a weenie," I told you. "You never do anything. You should run."

Deep into your nightclubbing phase, where I did not join you, because I was, as you explained, the most boring Saturday-night person on earth, you declined to train for a 5K. But you took vitamins; you stretched; you tried massage therapy.

An e-mail from a mutual friend broke the indisputable news you were too devastated to speak: You had multiple sclerosis.

MS is a disease that eats away at the myelin coating surrounding the nerves. It can affect balance, vision, even cognitive ability. People can be in a wheelchair within a year, or live until their 80s with no one ever knowing they have MS. Although it affects more women than men, by a ratio of 2 to 1, it affects women less seriously. And so we didn't think it would be so bad.

It was, though. It was so bad.

You had primary progressive MS, the worst kind.

Four years ago, I realized that this fierce little actor had never been to Broadway. And so we went, staying in a fancy hotel with our best sequined skirts and your walker, to see your favorite musical, *The Man of La Mancha*. As Brian Stokes Mitchell sang of the impossible dream, the unbeatable foe, the willingness to march into hell for a heavenly cause, I realized I could use my small measure of celebrity to try to raise money for something— more properly, for someone. You had helped me craft the heroine of my sixth novel, *The Breakdown Lane,* a dancer who lost her husband and got MS in a single, harrowing year. Beyond donating a portion of that book's sales, I could use it as a sword to fight a windmill dragon that remained tantalizingly out of reach.

A couple of years ago, at a speech in Washington, D.C., my twenty-second fundraiser for MS research, I was about to sign books when I heard the old Billy Withers song *Lean on Me*.

I looked up, and there on the screen, larger than life, was a photo of me with my head on your shoulder. I spattered the title pages with tears as the coordinator read a letter you had written. I remember part of it: "Jackie was popular, and I was the little caboose. But she chose me, included me, and when she learned I had MS, she jumped in to help me and to beat this disease. She is more than a friend. She's my heart."

That goes both ways.

You aren't my sister, but it would never occur to my children to call you by your first name. When my actor son, Marty, now twenty, graduated high school and was accepted into a Bachelor of Fine Arts program for Musical Theatre, he told me, "It's up to me, for Auntie too."

You have to lean on my arm when we walk now. But I have to lean on you, a hundred times a year, when I turn to you with problems no one else understands—or could accept. As you describe them, they're like locational humor: To get it, you had to be there.

You always are.

Love,

Jackie

two generations of non-girly girls

BY ROBIN TROY

ear Evaun,

When I hung up yesterday, I swore I would drive straight to Walgreens to print my photos so I could finally send you pictures of my daughter, Quinn. Every time we talk I say I'll do it, and every time I hang up, I get waylaid washing baby bottles or reading *Fuzzy Bee*, and another day passes. If only you had a computer, I could email you photos. The Walgreens is one mile from my house, right next to the post office. Quinn is almost five months old. I used to be a person who tackled her to-do list as soon as the sun rose, but now your address sits on a pad next to my computer—Missoula, MT 59808—while I sing *Hush Little Baby* around in circles, making up most of the words.

Motherhood changes things—but you've known this for a long time. Your son, Garold, is within striking distance of my seventy-one-year-old dad. I remember you telling me about

Garold waking you up to go to the bathroom in the middle of the night when he was a child. It was an outhouse in the backyard of your Bonner house, and you would call out to him in the freezing cold to make sure he hadn't fallen in. By the time I met you, your bathroom had been inside for decades, with the built-in toilet-paper-and-magazine holder you made yourself. I was twenty-nine and fifty years your junior when I first came to one of your parties, and I guess when I say that motherhood changes things I'm thinking less about unsent photos than I am about the day we became friends.

Remember the margaritas? Your friends had paid their dinner tabs and left, but you and I decided to stay at the restaurant for one more drink. What must the waiters have thought? We looked like grandmother and granddaughter, but there we were, ordering rounds of top-shelf margaritas (three each?) and talking about boys. Back here in Connecticut, I still get a kick out of telling people how we met—that if I hadn't moved to Montana from New York, hadn't become a reporter, hadn't been assigned a Christmas article about a seventy-four-year-old man in your seniors bowling league who had been dressing up as Santa and flying in a helicopter to remote towns for thirty-plus years, hadn't accepted his offer to join all of you for dinner one night after bowling, hadn't watched you telling your bawdy jokes and drinking your scotch and poking the sides of the handsome men at the table, hadn't stayed late to have margaritas with you, we wouldn't have become friends.

And yet, our hitting it off was a lot simpler than that. The truth is we became friends because we have something in common (besides our birthday): Neither of us is a girly-girl. We aren't into hanging out with packs of women. We like to get ready for a party, and go to the bathroom, by ourselves. We like the casual company of men; we're good at being friends with men, though we call them boys. And we prefer scotch to cosmos. Margaritas are as foofy as our drinks get.

But motherhood changes things, right?

The last time I saw you, two years ago, I was living with my now-husband, and you had broken up with a guy twenty years your junior. When we bellied up at Harold's Club in the afternoon, we did what we always did: talked about the ins and outs of boys and marriage and money and children and *life*. And when Garold's friends came around—and the older guys too—you lit them up with stories about their childhoods and with one of your jokes.

"You know why women have poor spatial relations? Because we're told twelve inches looks about like this," you said, holding your hands just a few inches apart.

You must have built up an arsenal of those zingers in all your years waiting tables.

There are never many women in Harold's. If we were there right now—with Garold on his stool at the end of the bar, making sure we didn't pay for one drink—I would confess to you this: Now that I am a mother, I am, for the first time in my life, seeking the company of women. Groups of women. For a change that feels so natural, it is also strange. Now, when my husband and I have couples over for dinner, the men talk to the men and the women talk to the women. We women sit in a separate room from our husbands, our conversations (fascinating to us) focused on boobs and poop. I'm sure you could come up with a good dirty joke about us. But would you and I have stayed late for margaritas if we'd met today? Now I have playdates with these packs of moms—our infants lined up on the floor, more aware of their teething toys than each other—and we talk and talk about mom-things, women-things that, well, our men aren't interested in. For new friends, we women have come to just about love each other just about overnight.

And sometimes I wonder where the old Robin has gone.

But more often, I am so glad I followed the advice you gave me at Harold's, over free desserts, in the red booth at Scotty's Table on our birthday, sitting in front of the fish tank in your condo after you sold your Bonner house: Marry someone you love, who *loves loves loves* you back. Be sure, also, that he makes some money. Then, *love love love* that baby. And, above all else, enjoy your life. Keep ripping and running. Don't be afraid to ruffle a few feathers. Have fun in this world.

I still have the framed, signed copy of your poem you gave me just before I got on the plane last time. Now it's on my desk:

Life begins with L.
Life itself is a beautiful thing.
It was given to us to enjoy,
So use it to the fullest.
L is for living.
L is for laughter,
L is for loving.
The 3 L's will carry you through
Life on a cloud of Happiness.

It reminds me of our trip to Browns Lake. Talk about clouds of happiness. The wind was whipping but the sun was strong, and we stood shin deep in the lake and asked strangers to take pictures of us, our arms around each other. You showed me the spot where you and your husband used to camp with your best "couple-friends," back when you were all raising your kids. I like to picture you laughing your heads off around campfires and cook-stove dinners—and I wonder if the men talked to the men and the women talked to the women on those nights. I wonder if you too reached a point, at my age, when you spent less time making handsome men laugh at your jokes and more time appreciating the company of women. It has been on my mind.

When we talked on the phone last week, you told me your friend Lou got engaged. She must be in her midseventies by now, with, what, seven children? And you told me you'd broken up with your boyfriend again. He sounded like a nice guy—a guy who loved your company, no surprise. But I got the impression that maybe he wasn't so spicy, didn't have enough kick for your taste. And this time the breakup sounded definite—not like the first few attempts, where you two had it out after bowling but then stayed around for an extra glass of whiskey to talk and talk some more, until he convinced you to stick with him a little longer. I told one of my students about your breakups. He's in his early twenties, and he's been trying to figure out whether or not to stay in a relationship with a very nice girl. I told him he'd better get used to these ups and downs—maybe even learn to enjoy them—since we apparently don't change as much as we think we will when we grow up. Funny, you and my student have a lot in common right now: living on your own, dating, going to parties, watching friends get married.

And here I am with all of my loose ends tied up: married, house, good job, first child, a whole bunch of new female friends. It's not that I think about a time when things will shift again, but my friendship with you shows me, every day, that it will happen. Quinn won't be thirteen pounds forever, same as you didn't live in your Bonner house with a fleet of hummingbirds in your backyard forever, same as I won't forever be seeking the companionship of women. But for today, I am a new mother. Today, my daughter likes to sleep with her head over my heart, not in her crib. Today, you are going to Butte with Lou and a group of friends—men and women—for a weekend house party. By next week, my daughter might love sleeping in her crib. By next week, you might call me up to tell me you just met a guy whose jokes are as clever as yours.

I ask my students, "Can you write a story about a perfect day? Would it be an interesting story to read?"

They're not so sure. They like to write about death and abuse and explosions—stories with juicy, blockbuster conflicts.

"Yes," I tell them, "you *can* write a good story about a perfect day, because that day is going to end." In the knowledge of that ending lies the tension, and it is the tension that, as you say, keeps us ripping and running.

I loved our picnic on the riverbank behind your condo. After talking about doing it for years, it was finally happening: you and me, down by the river, in a heat wave, the water rushing past us. No picnic for girly-girls, it was just as we had pictured it—baking sun, cold water, hard rocks beneath us and scratchy grasses in our hair, shielding us from the heat. We were two girls free of men or children, and we did what we always do—talked about boys and life. As perfect as our day was, I think both of us felt a little bothered by the fact that, once we hoofed it back through the tall grasses to your condo, we wouldn't have our first picnic to look forward to anymore.

Not that we won't have more picnics. The next one will be this July. It will be a different kind of picnic. You will meet my daughter. She will be almost eleven months old. You and I will be just shy of our next birthday. It is a day we talk about every time we call each other. And when we hang up, you go out dancing and I go back to showing Quinn how to roll over. You put on one of the snazzy blouses you made yourself and I go for days in the same fleece and leggings. I plan play dates, and you have an extra whiskey and let a nice guy charm you another time.

One day, yes, you and I will stay late and have margaritas again.

This morning, Quinn goes from her tummy to her back by herself. I reach for the phone to tell you, but it's still too early, Mountain Time. I want to talk to you. I have something on my mind. I want to tell you that this day is perfect: There is snow falling outside, my husband and daughter are downstairs, you are still asleep in the mountains—and our lives? They are our stories, and they are sparkling with tension.

Love,

Robin

not sometimes, but *always*

BY ANNA COX

ear Lara,

This morning I flossed my teeth and thought of you.

Not the poetry you were hoping for? Sorry, but it's true.

I met you in a miserable year of dental paranoia, death, and divorce. In a year when I kept closing in on myself, you quietly made space and simply said, You will be okay. In a year when I didn't think I could care about anything ever again, you taught me how to care. About myself. About you. About anything. Again.

Who knows why we connect with some people and not with others. Sometimes you get lucky and click with someone right away. Sometimes it takes a weird combination of painkillers, elastic-waist pants, and the loss of something so fundamental you feel like you've lost yourself. That is where our friendship began. With loss.

I t's dangerous to fuse the roles of husband and best friend into one person because when you get divorced you lose the two people too quickly. All at once your source for Friday night sex and Saturday morning brunch disappears. *Poof.* Suddenly you're at brunch alone, drinking coffee, surrounded by the bed-head couples that just did it and then decided to flaunt that fact in public, over eggs.

No sex and no brunch and no emotional comfort—that's the easy part, the stuff you expect. What inevitably splits you open is the sneaky stuff: not knowing what to do with your hands when you sleep; finding a Post-it note with his handwriting on it; realizing you don't have anyone to take you to the dentist.

I live in a small town, and I like to keep my private parts private, so all my medical scraping, be it yearly uterine or twice yearly dental, happens in the nearest big city, about an hour away. Getting a ride to the dentist was never a problem before, because my husband and I would go together. We coordinated our appointments mostly out of efficiency, but also partly out of love—my husband knew I didn't like the dentist, so he would go with me and make me laugh. Just knowing he was in the waiting room made the visits to the bad man at the bad place not so bad.

But this year was different. And by different, I mean bad. This year my father died, my two closest friends moved out of state, my husband and I divorced, and, oh yeah, I needed three fillings replaced.

I'd rescheduled the appointment multiple times and had even considered begging my mother to drive four hours just to haul her grown daughter to the dentist. The man I'd taken as my lawful wedded husband had taken off. Who's gonna take me to the dentist now?

Somehow at a small university, in an even smaller town, you and I had managed to exist in similar but unconnected circles—a Venn diagram waiting to be realized. During my first year at the university we served on the same committee. You seemed committed to this committee. I saw it as a gargantuan waste of time—a weekly drone fest where policy discussions ground to a halt because of misused semicolons. You took your job seriously and received a university teaching award. I wore a t-shirt that said, *Here I am, a victim of geography*. After one meeting I think I asked where you got your hair cut. That was the extent of our interaction. Like many women, I assumed that other women had it all figured out. Everything in your life seemed purposeful and polished. Why would you ever want to hang out with someone like me?

When I called you I wasn't looking for a friend; I was looking for a ride to the dentist. But before I had the chance to ask for a ride, you invited me to dinner. Your husband was out of town and you wanted some company.

That night, we sat at your kitchen table and drank bourbon and gingers. Your kitchen was a Williams-Sonoma arsenal of the newly married: shiny pots, panini press, three different devices for making coffee, a rainbow of assorted spatulas. My kitchen was haute divorcée: one fork, one spoon, one knife, lots of liquor. You've since told me I was charming that night. It must have been the bourbon. I'm surprised I was able to carry on a conversation at all given how most of the thoughts in my head were either boring despair or hopeful echoes of *everythingwillbe-okayeverythingwillbeokay.*

What could I have possibly talked about? When I wasn't working I was crying and when I wasn't crying I was thinking about crying and then it was time to go to work again. I'd recently begun two new activities: an academic study of the distilleries of the south (one bottle at a time) and waxing my own bikini area. This new skill set had reaped surprising collateral benefits. Armed with a stiff drink and a sharp exhale, I'd found I could do things I never thought possible. I kept those things to myself. I was drinking a lot those days.

Where is the Emily Post advice on asking a veritable stranger to fulfill a role your husband previously filled? Did that advice-slinging-know-it-all have no dental paranoia or no marital discord or no clue? I drained the bourbon and ginger that you'd just refreshed and before you could even put the cap back on the booze, I blurted:

"Will you take me to the dentist? I'm kinda freaked out and normally Marty would take me but, uh . . . you know, and I have to take drugs so I can't drive, and will you take me, could you take me? Please? I'd drive myself but I'll be drugged up and I can't drive. . . . I'll pay for gas . . . please?"

My voice cracked, but I didn't cry. If I had cried you probably wouldn't have cared. You're like all women—given the right time of the month you'll cry at television commercials full of arresting images like furry puppies schilling toilet paper. But I felt that if I lost it about the small stuff, then you'd see how really freaked out I was about my dad dying and my marriage dissolving. My veneer couldn't crack—it was all I had.

I doubt I was fooling you, but you were gracious enough not to call my bluff. Instead, you sat across the kitchen table and looked at me with the patience of someone who recognizes a vulnerable moment and has the good sense to tread lightly, or maybe you just looked at me with the fuzzy logic of someone who had matched me bourbon for bourbon.

"Sure."

The morning of the appointment, you were prompt (something that hasn't happened since then). We must have talked during the hour-long car ride, but if we did, I don't remember any of our conversation. In fact, I don't remember anything until I woke up in the dentist's chair and saw him leaning over me with his paper mask in my face and his latex fingers in my mouth. He turned my face to the side and leaned over me. He smelled good—like safety, like care. Maybe the bad man wasn't that bad. My face was close enough to his chest that I felt his warmth. I wanted to curl up in that dental chair and never leave. For the first time in many months, I didn't feel like I was in freefall. I was feeling safe. At the dentist?

"How are you?" he asked.

"I'm greeeeeeat," I answered. The *e*'s in *greeeeeeeat* forced my mouth into a druggy smile. Drool leaked from my mouth.

He helped me out of the chair and suggested I eat something to help me feel more normal. I must have said something like, "I haven't felt this good in months; I want to feel like this all the time. Normal sucks." I'd almost forgotten you were there until I heard you laughing, saying to him, "I'll make sure she eats lunch."

I needed soft food, so we ended up in an Italian place that used to be a pancake house. The decor was Las Vegas Venice meets IHOP. We sat in a red booth; I ordered noodles with spinach. Probably not the best choice, because I couldn't maneuver my tongue to remove the spinach that stuck between my teeth.

It felt oddly like a date: two strangers sharing a meal, trying to talk to each other. Would you tell me I had big chunks of green stuff stuck in my teeth, or would you pretend not to notice? I should be charming, I should talk . . . I should keep my head off the table.

The chatter in my head seemed smart enough, but what I actually said was:

Me: (slurring) When I look at you, I see two of you.
You: (practically) Then don't look at me.

After lunch we went to Target (or as we like to say, The Target), the first of many trips we would make there. (As our friendship progressed, we often went to Target—it became the symbol of our need, as two overworked women, to get the hell out of our tiny town and go look at shiny stuff that smells good.) Evidently the spinach-to-drug ratio wasn't titrated correctly, because I wandered off. You found me mesmerized, in front of a towering maxi-pad display. All that leak-stopping protection created a druggy epiphany. Protection. Not sometimes, but *Always*. Yeah.

You seemed to sense something was happening behind my glassy eyes, or maybe you were just afraid. Either way you calmly steered me from the Feminine Needs aisle and shepherded me through the checkout and into your car like your own very grown, very helpless child. (Hey, sorry about passing out in your car on the way home. Hope I didn't snore. Or drool. Or fart.)

For the next week, every time I flossed my teeth and saw my new white fillings, I thought about you. I felt a little less lonely, a little less bereft, a little less stuck in my spiral of suck.

Two weeks later you called early one Sunday morning.

"I can't pull up my pants."

"What?"

"I broke my wrist. I fell. I can't pull up my pants. I can't button. Can't snap. Can't zip. I need elastic-waist pants. All I have are ratty sweatpants; I can't teach in ratty sweatpants. Can I teach in ratty sweatpants? I can't teach in ratty sweatpants. How am I supposed to teach when I can't pull up my pants? Can you take me shopping? Please? I'll pay for gas . . . please?"

"Sure."

Whenever I'd seen you at work, you always looked so professional: smart, chic, and feminine. But that morning? Not so much. You answered the door with greasy hair, ratty sweatpants, your husband's used-to-be-white T-shirt, and a pilly fleece thing that was two sizes too big. The cast/sling contraption was so big that no sleeve would fit over it, forcing you into a perpetual state of undress. You were lugging around a full-sized bed pillow because you had to keep your arm elevated.

I helped you into the car and buckled the seatbelt around you like you were my own very grown, very helpless child. As I walked around the back of the car, I saw you lean your head back and swallow a painkiller. Pulling out of the driveway it occurred to me that I'd probably have to help you go potty. During the drive, you whimpered every time you rearranged your arm on the pillow. I wanted to pat your poor greasy head. We traveled on the very same road we had traveled two weeks earlier—only now, *I* was driving and *you* were drugged.

After an hour we arrived at Old Navy.

Oh, god. Old Navy.

Old Navy is the tequila of cheap clothes. It flirts; it cajoles. It convinces you it's your friend.

C'mon, what's another hoodie? It's only $5.

Sure, those pants fit. For five bucks anything fits!

You think you look great until it's too late, those pants *don't* look good, *nobody* needs that many hoodies, and you are too old for this shit.

Oh, god. Old Navy.

I grabbed about a dozen options off the racks and we lumbered to the dressing room. The teenage dude working there stepped back.

"Uh . . . like . . . uh . . . the handicapped one is the first one on the left."

"She's not handicapped, she's handi-capable, thank you very much." I snatched the number out of his hand. Six-garment limit, my ass.

I tried to organize the dressing room, and you tried to undress. You poor thing, you couldn't negotiate the tiny dressing room, your big pillow, your useless hand. You were getting frustrated.

Before that moment, I wouldn't have guessed it was possible. Two days prior, an award-winning, whip-smart academic.

Today a disheveled, drugged, pillow-lugging invalid shopping for pants that don't button, zip, or snap. In the horrible light of that Old Navy dressing room, I got it. You're like me. You try to do it all. All by yourself. It's not easy to ask for help. Most women are far better at helping others than, god forbid, asking for help. You and I had PhDs in helping others, but we were high school dropouts when it came to letting others help us.

I leaned down and took off your shoes like it was the most normal thing in the world. I tried to make you laugh by pretending to be a creepy physician:

"I'm going to touch you here now. . . . I'm going to take your pants off now. . . . Is this okay?"

We were cracking up in no time. As I guided your legs into pair after pair of ugly elastic pants, you tried your best not to drool on my head. You settled on two pairs of pants that, if you continued to knock back those painkillers, didn't look that bad and didn't make you look that pregnant.

But two pair of pants do not a wardrobe make, so we shoved the bag into the trunk and drove to Target.

You passed out in the car on the way home. I didn't care if you were snoring or drooling or farting. (You didn't fart.)

After the two drug-addled trips to Target, we began hanging out more regularly, but it wasn't until the end of that semester that we really articulated what our friendship was all about.

We were road-tripping to Philadelphia for a mutual friend's bridal shower. You promised to keep a drink in my hand if I promised to keep my mouth shut and not take bets on how long till the bridal bliss wore off.

It was nearly midnight, and we were stuck in bumper-to-bumper somewhere in Delaware. In the lane next to us there was a semitruck hauling medical waste.

I was trying to keep you awake.

"You know, I'm the kind of woman that reads the back of the tampon box and thinks, *Toxic shock?* Shit. How long did I leave that last tampon in? How long is too long? Is there still one in there? Did I forget to take my last one out? I mean, who forgets to take out their tampon, but maybe I just thought I did but I didn't, and is two hours too long? Because you know sometimes I get busy or I kinda forget; it's not that I *forget,* but I'm thinking about other things and then I realize, but maybe at that moment I just can't get to it, like I'm in the middle of the lecture and I'm supposed to be thinking about something else, but all I can think about is needing to get my tampon out. *Right then.*"

Oh, whoa. I'd just committed the classic roadtrip/one-night-stand mistake: confusing darkness with intimacy. I leaned my head against the window thinking about what exactly counts as medical waste and making sure the window was rolled up in case the truck jackknifed.

You turned toward me, and the medical waste truck, your voice a mix of relief and disbelief and said, "Oh. My. God. Me too."

And that night, in that dark car, on that crowded interstate, a magical light did glow.

In a miserable year of death and dental paranoia, broken wrists and drugged-up visits to Target and Old Navy, I found you, my Best Toxic Shock–Thinking Friend.

Most women are lucky enough to have a BFF (Best Friend Forever), but very few are lucky enough to have a BTSTF (Best

Toxic Shock–Thinking Friend). The BTSTF is the woman that magically appears at a particularly low or humiliating point in your life. She shows you that your particular brand of crazy is neither all that crazy nor all that particular. When you feel like you're the only freak in the room, she stands by your side—once a lone freak, now a freak army.

Our friendship was formed by extraordinary kindness in ordinary places and named with the verbiage of the feminine hygiene aisle. You stopped my hemorrhaging, you offered protection, you pulled the plug on my toxic-shock-worst-case-scenario-things-will-never-change-why-do-I-have-to-do-everything-myself thinking. You taught me that to pull myself together, I had to spread myself around.

You made a miserable year, a wonderful year.

Not sometimes, but *Always*.

Love,

Anna

Hi Leslie —
Thanks so much
for coming tonight.
Bevin Wallace

an ode to my partner in crime

BY BEVIN WALLACE

$\mathcal{D}$ear Lynne,

If you were sitting here with me tonight, we'd crack open some Boone's Farm Strawberry Hill and laugh so hard we'd pee our pants.

But you're not here, and I haven't laid eyes on you since 1984, not too long after high school. This seems impossible, since I still feel like a spazzy adolescent most of the time.

I don't think I realized until recently just how great, special—and hilarious—our friendship was. We're putting our house on the market, so I've been purging old boxes. And I came across our yearbook, *Ramblings '83,* and found the five pages (all marked SAVE FOR LYNNE at the top in red felt tip) you covered with doodles, silly quotes, inside jokes—and the memories came flooding back.

It made me realize that I haven't had a friend like you since. My daughter is only four now, but I can only hope she eventually finds a partner in crime, best pal, and "sister" who lives just up the block.

We learned a lot of lessons together. We did some bad stuff. We did a lot of things I think we should be a little embarrassed

about, but that's mostly because we thought the world of ourselves and truly believed that, with a little practice, one way or
another, we would be great, famous, rich or, preferably, all three.
(Remember our band? Our songs truly sucked, but we sure did
belt them out!)

We met in second grade. I can still picture you the day you
moved in down the street—arm in a cast and teeth crooked, just
like mine. But you had lived in Saudi Arabia and had a giant hoo-
kah pipe in your dining room, so clearly, you were very mysterious and sophisticated. We were immediately best friends.

Even though we had lots of separate friends, and I was preppy and you were punk rock (I attempted the New Wave look but
always had to incorporate a little pink or teal), we stayed best
friends throughout high school. It's not a lifetime, but those were
long years and, needless to say, eventful ones.

Some of my earliest memories revolve around dance and
gymnastics lessons at scary Miss Vicky's studio. Neither of us
was in any way a gifted dancer, and she always let us know it.
How old were we—eleven? twelve?—when she started busting
on us for drinking and/or hanging out with boys instead of training? (Which, alas, we totally *weren't* doing.)

Actually, I think my semislacker status started in those tum-
bling classes. Heck, if you're going to be called lazy and fat, you
might as well enjoy being them! And remember the recital cos-
tumes? The sequins, the feathers, the gaudy eye makeup expertly
applied by your mom? I think those experiences are what con-
verted us both into tomboys long before it was cool to be one.

And then there was our mean-spirited secret club (total
membership: two). Somehow we got it into our heads that we

were better (as in cooler, cuter, tougher, smarter) than the other girls on the block. And somehow we thought it would be a good idea to document those feelings—and our obviously excellent cartoon and graphic-art skills—in notebooks that we didn't hide very well. So maybe we were cuter, but we were definitely not smarter. I think one of the neighbor moms actually found one of our "spy books" under their trampoline—*oops*. I vaguely remember some humble apologies, and I pray those books were burned.

We had fleeting crushes on myriad neighbor boys. Remember sending my little sister into our house to ask the parents (who were always gathered around the bar at one house or another; why don't parents do that these days, by the way?) for an empty bottle so we could play spin the bottle? She wasn't really supposed to say what it was for, but then again, she must have only been about seven.

We loved that we looked alike, and we tortured our fifth-grade teacher by wearing similar outfits and switching seats. That amused us to no end. That and stealing the cute new boy's comb from the back pocket of his Levi's cords.

Our escapades in the "field" (now that I think about it, it was probably some kind of government cleanup site that sat behind our housing development) are another example of, well, adventurous spirits and toughness, but perhaps not intelligence. Three things stand out: our love of cattails; finding hundreds of 45 rpm records buried in a swamp of stinky, black muck and carrying them home on a broomstick; and carpeting our treehouse with asbestos-laden insulation panels. (They were so soft and fluffy! We itched for weeks.)

dolescence hit, and with that, braces (thank goodness) and the new, very cute neighbor, Keith. Did we love him or what! Remember how we used to watch for "movement" inside his house? And how if we saw any, we would burst into hysterical giggle fits and run and hide around the corner of your house? Then there was the time he was supposed to take us to Elitch's amusement park, and he blew us off. We sat in my basement (I think my mom was at your house, probably drinking martinis) drinking shots out of Dixie cups from my mom's vast and varied liquor assortment. I remember thinking we needed to call our moms because we were going to die. Luckily we passed out before we managed to get to the phone. While my first experience with drunkenness didn't exactly spare me from any future mishaps, it certainly taught me a lesson about not mixing tequila with vermouth.

We weren't meant to be gymnasts, but our many talents included: a blue ribbon–winning three-legged race (we practiced for weeks; it was the only time in my life that I didn't dread field day); doing The Hustle in very cool disco outfits in the sixth-grade talent show; our well-rehearsed middle school skit, called *The Streak* (I can still picture Julie running across the stage in that tan leotard); and, of course, our fabulous entry in the air-band competition senior year: *Let's Do the Time Warp Again.* We won. Finally, we were the celebrities we always knew we would be! Even if we couldn't write song lyrics like The Vapours or Big Audio Dynamite (but, man, did we try!).

hinking back on all this can sometimes make me sad that you are not in my life anymore, and then I start to want to blame someone (you, I guess) for not keeping in touch better.

After all, when you lived with us that summer before college, it really did feel like we were sisters. It didn't seem like we would need to even *try* to keep in touch, and we did see each other that first semester, when you were at CSU in Fort Collins and I was in Boulder. But then you transferred to a college in Florida and never came back. And really, I think the distance between us—you're still in Florida and I'm still in Colorado—is just too far. I mean, I can barely keep up with my friends who live a half an hour away!

But then again, maybe we were just meant to be each other's first best friend, the other half of all those silly childhood memories. This way, my memories of you, of us, will never be clouded by who we've become—for example, I don't know, or care, whether you're a Democrat or Republican. I don't know what kind of mother you are, or whether you eat junk food. In this adult world, who knows if we would even be friends if we lived next door to each other?

To me, you will always be the girl who knew me when I was becoming me. You had a big hand in helping to make me the person I am, for better or worse. So I'm not famous or rich, or even notorious. But I still think I'm pretty great. And I have you to thank for that.

Your beef (Ha! Remember that?),

the mother of all adventures

BY KATIE ARNOLD

To All My Fellow Adventure Girls,

I'm looking out my window at a perfect New Mexico day: The desert sky is china blue, with only the faintest wisps of high clouds, and the chubby piñons are doing a shy little rumba in the breeze. It's early March and 70 degrees. Oh, but winter will be back! Remember that May morning we woke to clumpy, fresh snow coating the foothills, like someone had dumped a giant batch of cream-cheese frosting on everything? I called you and we climbed Picacho, up through Glitter Canyon, the peak above all spackled and shimmery, an ice cream cone in the sun. Really, who doesn't love a fresh dumping of snow in May, when you know that summer is pounding on the door, impatient to get in, with her hot piney smells and those long, long, baking days?

But in case you hadn't noticed, things have changed recently. Now I spend my days as vigilant keeper of Pippa's nap schedule, listening to staticky repetitions of *Row, Row, Row Your Boat* (compliments of the lullaby CD wheezing through the baby monitor), hoping she'll keep sleeping and yet waiting for her to wake up so we can go for a hike. You see, the way I live best is outside, in the fresh air and sunshine, with my body in constant motion. Lugging a live, warm, snoring, fifteen-pound baby uphill is pretty heavenly, and there are times when I need to go solo to air out my brain, but there are many days when I miss you, my fearless girl gang.

I came to this realization a few weeks ago. I woke up craving a long, punishing mountain bike ride—the kind where you leave before breakfast and straggle home after dark, dirty and tired and content, not having given one single thought to what you'd left behind. Outside it was bright and wintry—no weather for riding—but something about the way the morning sun slanted through the windows reminded me of summer. I moped around all day, feeling sorry for myself, until Steve issued an order. "Go for a run," he said, which is Steve-speak for "Get lost and don't come home until you're in a better mood." I obeyed, and it was nearly dark as I was hurtling down the trail, trying to outrun the night, feeling happy and lonely at the same time, when it hit me: I love my adventure girls! I love that I can still call any one of you at short notice and find someone game enough to blitz up to the trailhead for a hike or a morning ski. I love all the things we've done together, spontaneous and ill-planned, bold, dumb, and glorious.

We learned to roll kayaks and cast flies together. We dug dummies out of the snow at avalanche school; watched the full moon set as the sun rose over Utah's Canyonlands; cranked through steep, dusty single-track in Idaho; paddled desert rivers on the longest day of the year; nursed heartbreak and flirted with surf instructors in Hawaii. When we were ten, we learned to sail in our soggy Tretorns, dragging each other onto the hull like waterlogged mink after the boat capsized. You convinced Steve and me to tag along on your backcountry honeymoon, and I talked you into going fly-fishing with me a week before Pippa was born. (In retrospect, one of my dumber ideas.) We've chased after-work mountain bike rides with margaritas, raced all night long in Moab, and spent entire long days swimming in the lake.

When I sliced my knee open on the trail and had to fashion a baggy little tourniquet out of my T-shirt, you were the first person I called from the hospital pay phone. I had just moved to Santa Fe and barely knew you.

"Uh, I fell while hiking and need a ride home?" I said lamely.

"I'm on my way," you told me, and when you walked into the waiting room, it was like seeing my oldest, dearest friend in the world. "Next time we'll go together," you said. And we did.

Together, we've had plenty of close calls, both real and imagined. We've nearly run over herds of grazing cows—big, slow, and scary when you're screaming downhill on your bike—and we've come across giant paw prints squished into the dirt, so fresh that I could sense the mountain lion about to slink out of the shadows and maul us.

Oh, and who can forget all the times we were caught out in thunderstorms and nearly electrocuted? (Exaggeration, maybe, but you know how phobic I am.) "Please take care of Gus," I begged you during one particularly lunatic mission, as we huddled with our bikes on a high ridge, trying to remember how not to get zapped: *Do you stand under a tree, or near a tree, or in the open? Do you lie flat or crouch with one leg in the air, to keep the current from forming a circuit? How is it that we still don't know this?* "Of course," you said magnanimously, even though you're allergic to dogs. "And you can have my car."

We've logged countless Saturday morning bike rides and subjected ourselves to stupidly cold winds and frostbite to ski thigh-deep powder just after sunrise. On one recent dawn patrol, I clomped out my back door in my ski boots, helmet, and goggles, my skis riding the knobby bump on my shoulder. It should be noted that it was not yet dawn, I was five months pregnant, and we were eighteen miles from the ski resort, in the middle of a still-sleeping suburban neighborhood. At first I felt strange and bloated and alien, but giddily so. Should someone look out their window, they'd see a shadowy skier lurching through the becalmed darkness on her way to meet her friend, who sat snug in her car with the heat running, head thrown back, laughing.

I most certainly would not have attempted to climb Half Dome—beloved icon of Yosemite, prize of rock climbers worldwide—had you not told me I could.

"It's easy. You're in great shape. You'll be fine!" you said breezily when I pointed out that I had gone rock climbing maybe half a dozen times in my life. Flattered, I foolishly believed you, and during the eight-mile approach hike, I was certain you had something else in mind: Perhaps you'd short-rope me up the face, literally haul my body weight to the top? You'd said we were going to "climb," but maybe you really meant "walk"? Was there an easy little hiking trail just around the corner? When we reached the base of the wall, I could see that I was gravely mistaken. A skyscraper of smooth, featureless granite—Half Dome!—yawned above us. You smiled reassuringly and told me to put on my climbing shoes. What followed was a blur of panic, disbelief, and elation, but I do recall you—the consummate climbing pro—cheering and belaying me 2,000 feet up the lumpy face of Snake Dike, wisely distracting me when I accidentally looked down and noticed that the giant fir trees had become tiny, prickly arrowheads far, far below. At the top, we split an orange and admired Yosemite Valley, emerald green and glinting in the sun, and just like that, this crazy thing I'd agreed to do became the greatest thing I've ever done.

Then there was the time we nearly set the historic ghost town on fire. Oh, I know, we'd been riding our bikes above tree line in Colorado all day, and we were cold from the rain, and we hadn't seen Steve or the sag wagon for hours—he had all our warm gear, after all—and the sky had cracked open like a rotten cantaloupe and pelted us with hail. So it was smart—ingenious even—when you plucked your miniature, never-before-used survival kit from your Camelbak, fished out a single wilted match, and proceeded to build us a campfire beneath the eaves of a decrepit building, circa 1890-something, in the once booming, now defunct mining town.

The rain had stopped, but we were chilled, annoyed, and (let's admit) a little bit bored. So out came the match and your Minnesota camp-girl pluck. We gathered scraps of sticks and pelts of moss and made a tidy pile. It lit right away, a narrow plume of smoke climbing into the sky. We put our palms to the warmth and sat back on our heels and felt flush with pride. Such intrepid, fearless girls were we! So skilled and self-sufficient! Hypothermia

averted, we settled in for a cozy, self-congratulatory chat, ris-
ing ever so often to absentmindedly stoke the fire with kindling
we'd foraged from the hillside. Did we accidentally throw on a
few pieces of rotten historic timber? No, not us. Far above, Steve
crept slowly down the switchbacks, magnetized by the smoke,
as though it were a cheerful beacon in a dark night. "The minute
I saw it, I was afraid it was you idiots," he told us later, after the
flames had been safely doused and the embers scattered and the
historic ghost town preserved, once again, for perpetuity.

When Pippa arrived, and my definition of adventure changed.
With a new baby in tow, I convinced myself that it was
easier to go solo than to subject you to the tiny, squalling squir-
rel affixed to my chest. I thought I had to figure out how to be a
badass backcountry mom all by myself—and that definitely *was*
the dumbest idea I've had to date. Because one day, when Pippa
was four months old, she and I passed a homeless man on the
trail. I nodded hello, but he only yelled, pulled a rock out from
behind his back, and hurled it at my head. I remember feeling
outraged—*Who pegs people with rocks?*—and then a sharp, jagged
pain pulsed above my left temple. He started to yell and chase us,
and I had only time to run—not think—and fast.

Later, after I pulled Pippa from her carrier, still wide-eyed
and silent, like a baby owl plucked from the nest, and after the
ER doctor stitched me up, we went home and I tried not to think
about what had happened—what could have happened. In the
calculus of adventure, what was missing was you. Since then,
I've been flooded again with your invitations and companionship; new friends and old who show up for ski tours and hikes

with miniature poodles and five-month-old babies. We swap much-needed pep talks about life, love, and work, and if I bore you to bits with Pippa's sleep schedule, you never let on. You give what I need most: your time and love and a game and happy confidence that's utterly, perfectly contagious.

What I've learned, then, is this: Being with you isn't better than being with boys or husbands or babies or myself. It's just different. There's no competition, only an unspoken pact to laugh as much as possible and to push ourselves and each other to be better, stronger, braver, and sillier than we'd be on our own. Having adventures without you is only half the fun.

Oh good, Pippa is awake—we're going hiking! See you at the trailhead in an hour!

Love to you all,

Katie

who needs pink ribbons with a friend like you?

BY ALICE LESCH KELLY

ear Kate,

You were the first friend I told.

You were waiting for my call. You knew about the lump, about the doctor visit, about the look of concern on my doctor's face when he examined my breast.

"It's probably nothing, right?" I asked him.

He waited just a little too long to answer.

"Probably," he finally said, drawing out the word. "I'd like to get a better look at it." He picked up the phone, called the hospital, scheduled an ultrasound—and a biopsy, if necessary—for the next day.

"He made the appointment himself?" you said. "That's a bad sign."

Two days later, he gave me the news.

"I'm sorry. It's cancer."

I barely knew you when you had cancer a couple of years earlier. Our sons were in the same kindergarten class but had not yet become pals. One of the other mothers told me about you. She said you had Hodgkin's disease—or was it Non-Hodgkin's? Some kind of lymphoma.

"That poor woman," I thought.

Little did I know.

A few months later, our boys started playing together, and we became friends too. By then you had finished your treatment. Your hair was growing back. While the boys hit baseballs and ran around the yard, you and I drank tea and relayed our life stories.

I waited a long time before asking you about your cancer. I thought it would upset you. I didn't know then that what's upsetting is when people ignore it, not when they bring it up.

During my treatment, friends and neighbors were amazing. They brought cookies, fresh-picked strawberries, ice cream, and bottles of homemade fudge sauce. They took care of my kids on chemo days and invited them to movies. They sent gifts—DVDs, books, chocolate, a silk scarf for my bald head.

And they sent flowers—so many flowers.

I felt guilty for hating the flowers. But they made the house smell like a funeral home. You understood that. You told me it was okay to put them all in the garage.

I had eight chemotherapy treatments over the course of four months. After each one, you did something I will never forget. You called me every day—every single day—to ask me how I felt. When other people checked in, I downplayed the nausea, fatigue, and depression. I felt I had to protect them from the truth. But I told you everything. And you never flinched.

Everyone offered to cook meals, but you managed it all. You organized an email list and figured out a schedule so that we wouldn't end up with five dinners on one night and none the next. You reminded people to bring food in disposable containers so we wouldn't have to worry about washing and returning stacks of casserole dishes. You even made copies of some of my family's favorite recipes and told people who should bring what. You knew from experience that if you didn't, everyone would make lasagna.

After I finished treatment, you and I started taking walks— slowly at first, because I was weak. But I regained my strength, and we logged quite a few miles. My hair started growing back, and I packed away my bandanas.

Walking around the neighborhood, we both looked perfectly healthy. Anyone would have thought we were two women without a care in the world, chatting about fluffy stuff like our kids' baseball games and our vacation plans and what color to paint the living room. Sure, there was some of that. But mainly we talked about things that women in their early forties shouldn't have to think about—things we couldn't discuss with anyone else.

We talked a lot about dying.

We each had a pretty good prognosis. But with cancer, you never know for sure whether you've made it to the end zone. Favorable statistics and clean scans offer hope but no guarantees. The longer you're cancer-free, the better your odds of beating it, but you're never out of the woods—it can come back at any time. The words "metastasis" and "incurable" never lose their power to terrify.

During the few years since your diagnosis, you'd made some peace with the fear. But it was all new to me. It consumed me sometimes. And you understood that.

You understood why I agonized over every headache, cough, or sore muscle, worrying that my cancer had spread to my brain, lungs, or bones.

You understood why I needed several glasses of wine and an Ativan to get to sleep the night before an MRI or mammogram.

You understood why I cried at my son's third-grade recorder concert.

And you assured me that I too would make some peace with my fear. But it would take a while, and that was okay.

We found so much common ground. We both hated—*hated*—when people said that cancer happens for a reason. It doesn't. Or that cancer is a blessing in disguise because it clarifies your priorities. It isn't. Or that God won't give you any more than you can stand. Don't get me started on that one. Or that whatever doesn't kill you makes you stronger. No. Even if you survive, cancer weakens you, because it steals a part of you that you will never get back, no matter how strong you become. Nobody with cancer comes out ahead.

And then there were the ribbons. You listened so generously as I ranted about the whole pink-ribbon thing. Can't I buy cream cheese without being reminded of all this? Does the world really need breast cancer Tic Tacs? And why in the name of Susan G. Komen would someone buy a pink stand mixer? I know those damn ribbons help raise money for research, but it pisses me off that corporate America is exploiting my disease to sell chicken noodle soup, vacuum cleaners, chocolate, mascara, T-shirts, beach towels—even wine. Breast cancer wine! Don't they know that alcohol raises the risk of breast cancer? What's next, pink-ribbon cigarettes?

A few months after I finished my treatment, you called and asked if I wanted to go for a bike ride. It was one of those unexpectedly warm and sunny early spring days that makes everyone in New England giddy. I hadn't been on my bike in probably a year. When I dug it out from behind a jumble of lawn chairs and flowerpots and soccer balls and a four-foot-high plastic snowman in my shed, I could have written my name in the dust on the seat.

We headed over to the bike path near the river but gave up on it when we discovered that it was crowded with people gorging on sunshine.

We dawdled around on neighborhood streets for a while but had to keep dodging cars.

"Let's go to the cemetery," you said.

It was deserted. Clumps of purple and yellow crocuses had begun blooming, even though there was still some old snow on the ground. The tree branches were bare, but if you looked closely, you could see tiny leaf buds. For the first time in months, we felt the sun's warmth.

We rode to the top of a long hill.

"Let's ride down as fast as we can," you said with a grin.

You took off, and I followed. You pulled your feet off the pedals and stuck your legs out as you raced past rows and rows of tombstones, past the dearly departed mothers, the loving fathers, the beloved babies. Your hair, now long, flew in all directions.

You let out a shout. I couldn't hear what you were saying, so I sped up next to you.

You had a huge smile on your face as you soared down the hill.

"WE'RE ALIVE!" you shouted. "WE'RE ALIVE!"

I laughed, and then I joined in.

"WE'RE ALIVE! WE'RE ALIVE! WE'RE ALIVE!"

And four years later, we still are.

Thanks for showing me the way, Kate.

Love,

Alice

fireflies

BY MICHELLE GOODMAN

ear Stephanie,

When you first friended me on Facebook, I didn't want to accept. But within hours (okay, minutes), curiosity got the better of me, and I caved.

I'm embarrassed to admit that initially I was more interested in whom you were friending from high school and what you were writing on their Facebook walls than in seeing how beautiful your daughters were, or reading about where you worked or what you and your family did for fun on Sundays. For weeks, each time I'd log into Facebook, I'd check our Mutual Friends list to see which high school pals we had in common—and whether you too had friended Ronnie.

I know that concerning myself with whether you're sending instant messages and classic-rock quizzes and virtual pitchers of beer to a guy you tried to steal from me when we were sixteen probably makes it sound as though I need to get a better therapist—or at least get out of the house more. But you know when you go visit your mother and some little part of you reverts back to your teenage self? You cross your arms, roll your eyes, and argue with her about something insanely trivial, like whether the color she painted her living room is pale blue or faint gray?

That's what happened to me when I got on Facebook and saw all those blasts from our hash-smoking, Zeppelin-worshipping past. Suddenly it was like we were back in our mullets, feather earrings, and Jordache jeans that required a pair of pliers to zip up. Suddenly I was holding out hope that my Romeo in parachute pants would run his fingers not through your helmet hair, but through mine. Suddenly the most important item on my daily to-do list was Seeing Whether Stephanie Had Friended Ronnie On Facebook Yet.

It was as though I'd never spent a year reunited with Ronnie once the two of you stopped hooking up behind my back that miserable summer. As though I never made some semblance of peace with your lack of admission or apology. As though I never graduated from high school, moved away to college, moved on from Ronnie, and moved on from you. As though the past two decades of paychecks, bylines, U-Hauls, landlords, mortgages, pets, potlucks, friendships, funerals, new loves, and new heartaches never happened.

Instead, every time my Facebook feed told me that you made a new online friend or posted a photo of yourself, I'd be right back in my shag-carpeted Jersey bedroom, hiding under my sleeping bag so my parents couldn't see the light escaping from the push buttons on my phone, dialing and redialing first

Ronnie's number, then yours, sobbing to the endless busy signal until 3:00 AM.

Of course my ridiculous obsession with your Facebook friends list wasn't just about your refusal to fess up when I begged you to admit that you were the one he'd been burning up the phone lines with night after night. It wasn't just about the borrowed boyfriend.

It was also about the borrowed dad.

I know there are more remarkable things in life than two married couples who spend Saturday nights, vacations, and holidays together, then divorce within a couple years of each other, only for a new couple to emerge from the rubble. Hell, I have friends who've done the same thing. (They're the age our parents were back then.) But when you're sixteen, it's hard to imagine anything more unsettling than your dad packing his suitcase, moving into his own apartment, and—within weeks—openly dating your best friend's mom, especially when your best friend has already helped herself to your own boyfriend.

Since your parents were the first to get divorced, I figured you of all people would understand why my dad bringing along your mom on one of our earliest postseparation Sunday outings—and seeing him curl his arm around her hip all afternoon—was beyond disturbing.

Instead, you understood that telling me my dad had been buying you presents and would be spending Thanksgiving with you, your mom, and your sister would ruffle my feathers. And I understood that the carcass of our friendship was officially cooked.

Sure, we'd still share many of the same friends junior and senior year. We'd even chitchat idly in the high school parking lot or at parties from time to time. But damned if I was ever going to dial your number, confide in you, or trust you again.

Until I wrote this letter, I thought my freakish preoccupation with your Facebook comings and goings was about me holding the world's longest grudge. I'd see that sunny avatar filled with your blonde curls and smooth skin and think, *Skank!*

I thought I would blast you here for having the empathy of a garden snake. I thought, *Me, good. Skank, evil.* Total teenage black-and-white thinking.

But twenty-five years have passed, and my memory's become a bit hazy. It occurs to me now that maybe I only heard what I wanted to hear. Maybe you weren't trying to rub our parents' rebound romance—fleeting as it was—in my face. Maybe you were trying to talk to me about the weird-ass "Are we gonna be stepsisters?" situation we found ourselves in, but all I heard was "Sucka! Look who's got your Daddy now!"

Maybe I was just as heartless when some guy who made you swoon dumped you, or when your own parents split up, and this was payback. Maybe once we outgrew playing dress-up in your sparkly fuchsia and lemon ballerina tutus and discovered boys, bongs, and John Henry Bonham, you decided you didn't like my company anymore but played along—and then played with my head—because it was easier than walking away.

But I don't really buy any of those reasons. I buy that we were typical suburban teens, coping with boredom and loss and loneliness the best we could.

Eight years ago I wrote this god-awful short story, not so loosely based on me and you. It was filled with banalities like, "One person's feelings always get sacrificed in the name of another's desires." And, "The more you love someone, the easier hatred comes when they double-cross you."

If I had to rewrite that story now, I'd ditch the *All My Children*-esque attempts to paint the protagonist as the scorned saint, the antagonist as the devious villainess, and the fickle men as hapless saps ruled solely by the dull throb in their pants. Because that's not our story.

Our story is about chasing fireflies barefoot through dewy grass on a perfect August evening, our white cotton little-girl nightgowns flapping about our scabbed knees. It's about getting yelled at by my mom for prancing around my bedroom half-naked with her scarves and lingerie hanging off our scrawny frames. It's about telling our little sisters to scram, building forts out of blankets and folding chairs, and staying up half the night giggling about god knows what. It's about me telling you the doll you gave me for my seventh birthday was ugly and you calling Mark Whatshisname from Hebrew-school carpool to tell him I liked him while your next-door neighbor pinned me to the ground and shoved a sock in my mouth.

It's about ribbing each other about who'd get their period or need a training bra or make out with anything other than our respective pillows first. Thinking John Belushi was Shakespeare and Cheech and Chong's *Up in Smoke* was still funny after seventeen viewings. Mixing pitchers of screwdrivers in the scorching summer sun, slathering ourselves with baby oil, and cooking our pink skin to a red, blistery crisp. Listening to the same Stones song for three hours straight, as if sheer will could make Mick and Keith materialize right then and there in your bedroom. . . . I could fill up an entire yearbook with hilarious, ridiculous, bittersweet memories.

In that short story I wrote about us almost a decade ago, there is one scene I'd keep—a scene that actually happened. We were in our midtwenties, at a mutual high school friend's wedding in the country. The ceremony wasn't set to start for hours, so a few of us saddled up to the hotel bar for cocktails. But within minutes it seemed, everyone disappeared, claiming dresses to iron, hair to curl, kids back home to call. That is, everyone but you and me.

I remember thinking, *Oh, crap!* and running through the list of plausible excuses I could use to slip upstairs (tampon, migraine, hemorrhoid, skank). Except I didn't slink off to my room. And it wasn't just because I had another $9 Bloody Mary on the way. We hadn't seen each other in six or seven years, now that there were 3,000 miles between us—me on the West Coast, you on the East. And once again, I was curious—about what you were up to, what on earth you might say to me, and whether the glue that once held us together would still stick.

There may have been awkward pauses. Or small talk about which classmates had already divorced, gone to jail, been killed by the mob. All I remember is you asking me the $64,000 question: whether I thought my father and your mother had gotten together before my parents split up.

It would be too easy to dismiss you as taunting me. I have to believe you were genuinely as befuddled as I was about painful endings, shocking beginnings, and the way the world can slip off its axis ever so slightly when the one thing you think is stable in life—your parents' marriage—proves anything but. I have to believe that like me, you wanted answers. A connection. Maybe even some sort of resolution.

I didn't want to give you any of that then. I was angry, and not just at you, but at our parents. So I told you I didn't know, downed my drink, and skedaddled.

If I could relive that scene today, I would have lingered at the hotel bar a bit longer. And not just to shoot the breeze about the people we graduated with who'd struck it rich, had six kids, or fallen from grace. But to really talk. I wouldn't have had many answers to share; not about our families, anyway. All I could have offered was what was in my heart: a girl who was sorry she had lost her oldest childhood friend. And then I would have raised my glass to yours and toasted those two little girls in white cotton nighties zigzagging across perfectly manicured lawns in the waning evening light, each of them clasping a mason jar filled with fireflies.

Your Facebook friend,

Michelle

air mail

BY DIMITY McDOWELL

ear Elizabeth,

I know, I know. It's been way too long. Like nearly three decades too long. And it must seem strange that I'm writing you a letter, because during our six-year friendship, we never once traded notes, as BFFs usually do. There was no need though: We were always pretty much either glued together or talking on the phone.

Not that we really had many deep phone conversations back in those days—after all, we were only five years old. I was allowed to answer the phone ("McDowell residence. May I ask who's calling?"), but I wasn't really old enough—or interested enough—to call my kindergarten friends. Yet just once a day, right before dinner, my mom let me dial your number (473-8182, which happened to be the number from which I was calling), and we'd talk for three whole minutes.

They were, if I remember correctly, pretty one-sided conversations. You weren't exactly a chatter. I liked to think that you preferred to listen to me. But maybe you just didn't like talking over the busy signal.

Thinking back, I realize it was odd that I called you right before dinner, since after all, you always ate with us. As I laid out the plates and forks, I was sure to count six places: one for Mom, Dad, my sisters Megan and Sarah, you, and me. Since BFFs naturally sit next to each other, your place was always next to mine. I tried to be the one to set the table every night and not leave the task for Megan, who refused to set a place for you.

"She's just a dumb imaginary friend," Megan would say. Then I'd get teary, and you'd slip off to a closet for a breather. You weren't one to lose your composure.

My mom would quickly remind Megan that we don't use words like "dumb" in our house, and, more importantly, that if I thought you were real, you were. So Megan would sulk around and sloppily throw your fork on top of your napkin, and not even pour you milk. I'd pick up her slack and fill your red plastic cup halfway, and then I'd scoop a little bit of mac and cheese or hamburger-spinach casserole onto your plate. I know you never had a huge appetite—and Lord knows, I understand why you didn't want to touch the casserole—so I didn't want you to feel like you were wasting your dinner.

So you didn't talk. And you didn't eat either. But you were clearly, clearly there.

Do you still have beautiful long hair? Your shiny, straight hair was the perfect length for pigtails, braids, or French braids— which, for me at the time, was the epitome of beauty. It wasn't short, with cowlicks splaying up everywhere, like mine was. I jammed barrettes in my hair to tame the sprouts, but it didn't really help much. Your hair, though, was exactly what I thought a girl's hair should look like, and it was as long as your beautiful name, which I just loved repeating: E-liiiiz-a-beth. Nobody ever mispronounced *your* name, asked you where it came from, or remarked, "How unusual" in a tone that inferred, "Why would you ever name your child that?" I often wondered how complicated the process of changing your birth name was. What I would've given to be an Elizabeth or an Amy or a Katherine. Anything but a Dimity (and definitely not a Dimitri, as I was often called.)

With your lovely locks, feminine name, and stunningly average height (you didn't tower over all the boys and girls in the class, as I did my entire life), you were never mistaken for a boy—which, as you know, also happened to me pretty regularly. Not bold or witty enough to respond, I would feel my cheeks freeze in embarrassment. More protective friends would yell back, "She's *not* a boy," then resume their play or addition tables, not noticing how jolted I felt. But then you'd appear (which was rare for you to do when I was in school) and reassuringly stand next to me. I could tell you knew I was holding back tears, how much it hurt my feelings to be categorized as a boy when what I wanted more than anything was to look just like you.

I don't mean to sound like a victim—after all, there are much worse fates than being tall, short-haired, weirdly named, and not terribly feminine-looking—but my narrow lens, then focused exclusively on Schumann Elementary School, didn't zoom out past my school bus route.

Are you any more strong-willed than you were back in the day? Not that I'm trying to put you down or anything—I mean, a girl could not have asked for a better friend. You were my enthusiastic pupil for endless hours in schools that were as magical as you were. We stumbled around in stilt school, seat-dropped endlessly in trampoline school, got dizzy in cartwheel school, and plunked out *Heart and Soul* ad nauseum in piano school. You happily took my tips on form, never huffing off in disgust. ("Point your toes, Elizabeth, when you seat-drop," I'd remind you for probably the fourteenth time that day. Or "Pianissimo, Elizabeth," I'd say with a tsk as you tapped the keys. "That means 'softly' in music.") You never complained about my television choices, squeezing in next to me to watch everything from *Sesame Street,* in the first year of our friendship, to *Little House on the Prairie,* my favorite during fourth grade. You played dollhouse and Operation, dress-up and Go Fish, never, ever suggesting we should do something else. I talked and talked at you, never once realizing how bizarre I must have looked and sounded, because you were as real to me as the friends my mom picked up in her wood-paneled station wagon.

I still can't believe I was lucky enough to have you as my friend.

I'd like to think that our friendship, like many I've had in my life, simply ran its course. It happens. One minute, you're enjoying each other's company, and then, for some reason—a move to another state, an overly demanding job, an annoying husband, too many kids and not enough time—you just part ways. Not that I had such massive challenges in fifth grade, of course. But in my defense, I did get busier as I got older, with tennis lessons, summer camp, French horn in the school band, weekends at my dad's house. (Funny to think that you and I were close to divorcing when my parents actually did!)

But I suspect you knew the real reason why I stopped calling you. Fifth grade meant middle school. Recess was a thing of the past, and our lockers had real, spin-'em combination locks. I was growing up, and I definitively knew that fifth-graders do *not* have imaginary friends. I became greedy in my quest for friends, dropping everybody, including you, who I deemed not worthy. I wanted to be "in" with the in crowd, not have one imaginary friend—even if she was prettier and cooler than anybody else in school.

I cringe now at how shallow I was, but my proverbial lens was still embarrassingly self-focused. All I thought mattered was wearing Guess jeans, sitting at the see-and-be-seen lunch table (where the occasional eighth grader would stop by to be adored), and being invited to the right slumber parties. I didn't need a nonjudgmental, amazing friend like you, Elizabeth; I wanted my friends to be queen bees, catty and cocky, in the hopes that their self-assured natures would rub off on me.

Not surprisingly, they didn't. In my quest to be popular, I ended up feeling more lonely and self-conscious than I'd ever felt. I knew, but would never admit at the time, that I would've much rather been teetering around with you on stilts on a Friday night than playing Truth or Dare at Laura's house, not knowing whether my "friends" daring me to prank call Ted to tell him I liked him would even acknowledge me on Monday.

So I guess this letter is to apologize for dropping you so suddenly and thoughtlessly. I'm sorry. If it's any condolence, I think of you often. I would've thought that marriage to my best friend, two kids, and nearly thirty years' distance between now and those painful middle school years would make me no longer covet the approval of the cool kids; would make me feel thrilled to stand taller than almost everybody I know; would make me feel secure enough to stand alone at a party and not worry about what people are thinking about me. And, for the most part, I have embraced the person I've turned into. To wit: My posture is as good as it's ever been; I have never grown out my hair (no patience for it, frankly); and I often pull a Madonna, introducing myself only with my funky first name.

But my cravings that led me to discover you—unconditional and, to be honest, unimaginable friendship—can still be ruthlessly stirred up with a sideways glance, an awkward conversation, or sheer lack of acknowledgment. It's those times I wish I still had your quiet presence in my life.

I can usually get over my self-consciousness to actually dine alone, something I never would've done in my twenties, or—heaven forbid—in middle school. But, just so you know, I'd like it a lot more if you were sitting across from me.

Your friend always,

Dimity

what comes true

BY DIANA ABU-JABER

ear Ferial,

You once told me—years ago, when we were both in graduate school—that you'd always felt there was something "a little bit selfish" about people who never had children.

At the time, I suspected that I was just that selfish. You remember what my father was like—training his daughters to be caretakers, to cook, open the house, invite the world in. The problem, though, is he didn't teach us that sometimes you have to close that door.

So I mostly spent my childhood watching children: I was raised around a lot of kids—younger siblings and cousins—in an extended family in an immigrant community. Maybe that's why I started writing, to hear myself think. That was me at bowling alleys and amusement parks, trying to write, ignoring the thunder of children and rides. You used to tease me about my "half-mindedness"—my half-listening or half-watching.

I'd sensed that one day I'd have to make a choice: children or writing. I'd grown up in a world of limited resources, never enough time or money for much beyond immediate necessities. For my hard-working parents, that meant there was just enough to keep the family going. For me, there would be just enough for my work.

Remember our study breaks in college? How we'd plan our futures? I'd seized on the dream of writing so long ago that my personality curved around it and grew into it. You, on the other hand, were ambivalent about school but clear about your other dreams: a house and family.

It's been years since we've talked, and last I knew, you had a house and career. But the part you wanted most, the husband and children, hadn't materialized. You were so clear about your desires, I'd always assumed they would certainly come true. I don't understand why they didn't. These days, I sometimes wonder about what really keeps us from our deepest desires—is it the unseen obstacle out there in the world? Is there perhaps some wisdom in us that knows the dangers of our dreams?

I sold my first manuscript when I was thirty years old. I'm a slow, laborious writer—it takes me forever to work out a plot, and there were endless revisions and sleepless nights. I needed all my hours, all my focus, to produce a book. Throughout my thirties, I was consumed by work, thrilled by it. I gave readings and talks; I wrote more novels, a memoir, another novel. . . .

But somewhere along the line, something changed. I turned forty and started to want more. I read a biography of a famous writer and learned that her greatest regret in life was that she'd never had kids. These words gave me a chill of recognition. At my readings, people asked if I had kids: I felt increasingly sad each time I said no. One day, someone in the audience answered for me, saying, "Her books are her children." At that moment, I realized: I didn't want my books to be my children.

By then, I'd almost convinced myself it wasn't possible for me. But the longer I've lived, the more I've been astounded by the mutability of identity. The facts of our lives suddenly swerve—names, bodies, careers change overnight. After years of thinking of myself as childless, child-free, the eternal auntie, I discovered midway through my forties that I might just be someone's mother too.

So Feri, I'm writing you with joy and confusion and fear and pleasure and all sorts of things, but not regret. And it's still hard to write you this letter: I recall too well how, over the years, every time a friend announced a pregnancy, I felt those drops of envy and grief.

I guess this letter is not only to tell you about our new little daughter, but to ask your forgiveness as well. Because I didn't know what I wanted, and you did, and things still didn't turn out like we expected.

When I play with our daughter now, I think about the pure, dumb luck of life. Questions answered that we never knew we'd asked. I'm so used to only having old dreams. I suppose part of me is worried about whether I've earned this new one. But who knows what's earned and what isn't? Perhaps the gifts we're most deserving of are the ones we never ask for at all.

With love and hope for all of your happiness and all of your dreams,

butt paste, bass, and beyond: an on-the-road friendship

BY JENNA SCHNUER

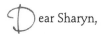ear Sharyn,

Writing a letter to you feels strange. In the five or so years we
knew each other, the written word didn't play a big role in keeping in touch—kind of funny, since we knew each other through
travel-writing circles. Come to think of it, we really didn't keep
in touch at all. Ours was one of those friendships where you just
know the other person is out there, and that you'll eventually
see her again. But day-to-day (or even month-to-month) contact?
Not our thing.

So when I found out you were gone, I was surprised how
much I missed you. After all, we spent, what, fifteen days together over the last five years? Most would consider that little
more than an acquaintance, but not us. No, we were on-the-road
family.

As travel writers, we both took trips where short-term bonds
(or annoyances) with other travelers were formed and, back at

the airport, left behind. Yet from the get-go—tooling around
Traverse City, Michigan—our friendship had a solidity to it that
easily surpassed friendships with people I had known for years.
I knew that if either one of us was stuck two hours away from
the other's home in a snowstorm, we'd find a way to show up
and whisk the other person to warmth and hot chocolate (unlike other friends, who we might just send text directions to the
nearest hotel).

Even when we saw each other, it wasn't like we sat down
and had big conversations about life's trickiest issues. We really
didn't even talk about the little details of regular life all that much.
I knew you were married, but if you had quizzed me about your
husband's name, I would have failed miserably. I have no idea
what foods you liked most, or which way you leaned politically.
Those details didn't matter to our friendship.

Because what I did know was how to crack you up. I knew
that you liked little side comments and a bit of snark. Now that
I think about it, that's probably why our friendship was so important to me. It was based on taking the piss out of each other.
It was a refuge from life's little annoyances (and, if I'm being
honest, the stupidity of others). I knew that I could always turn
to you to make fun of this or that, and that you'd think it was
funny. Even if I was poking fun at you. (Thanks for not smack-
ing me when, after learning you were a big-time fisherwoman, I
started calling you The Bassmistress. In public.)

And when you ribbed me about, well, *everything*, it was comfort. Hell, I actually enjoyed when you gave me the what-for—
usually in the form of a quick look or dry comment. You usually
did it at the world's most inopportune moment, like when I was

deep into a conversation I clearly didn't care about with another person. It was a task and a half to keep myself from laughing, but I always enjoyed the challenge of it. There was no cruelty to you.

I hope you felt the same way about me.

A few months ago, a mutual friend—a member of our "road family"—emailed me to tell me that after a brief but fierce illness, you had passed away. Some might find that cold but, really, it was a kindness. You gone? It seemed impossible. I don't think I would have actually understood her words if she had told me by phone. I read the message over and over. It didn't make any sense. You were always going to be there.

I 'm tempted to say that I wish we had kept in touch day-to-day while you were still here. But I'm pretty sure you were a no-regrets kind of girl. So I'll honor that and try to live as you lived. Full on. You weren't somebody who needed life's crap to remind you of how to live. You just plain old did it. But I will always keep the three emails I have from you—two are silly little one-liners about work stuff. Stuff I'd normally discard if I kept my inbox empty. (I don't, and I'm happy for that.) But the third—with a subject line of "can never have too much Boudreaux's [Butt Paste]"—well, that one I'm tempted to frame. I can't even remember why we started joking around about the product, but from that first trip on, it was all either of us had to say to get the laughing going. How I wish I could respond to your closing—"I hope to see you on the road. It's been way too long!"—with a "Yeah, see you soon!"

the end of the september–may romance

BY MAGGIE LAMOND SIMONE

ear Fellow Preschool Moms,

May is here, my friends, and I think we all know what that means. It is the end, once more, of the preschool year. The end, once more, of prescheduled two-and-a-half-hour chunks of time when things get done. And the end, once more, of mommy's social life.

And no, you cynics out there, I did not go out and party every day after dropping my girl at the door of the school. That is so out of line, really. Everyone knows that a mother's social life has nothing to do with—well, excitement of any sort. A "party" to me is a conversation with someone who understands my life, my experience, and the fact that I'm always just this side of a nervous breakdown. Now *that's* a good time.

For the last five years of preschool (between two late-year children), I have unfailingly become friends with—and sometimes, close friends with—many of you other moms dropping off your kids. It's easy to see how this could happen. How could we not? Every day, twice a day, for months on end, we stand there in a small space together waiting to drop off and pick up. I defy any mom to go a month, let alone an entire school year, without "falling in like" with one of the other moms.

I'm telling you, it can't be done. (And Kim, don't you shake your head out there. Sure, you were a tough nut to crack, but you know by the end of that year you found me irresistible.)

So we become friends, and our kids become friends. (We let them think they did the choosing—it's kind of a mommy secret.) We have playdates, during which we moms have coffee and bagels and cinnamon rolls and talk about life and love and childcare issues while our children busily do whatever it is they do on playdates. (Frankly, we don't care. As long as we hear no crashes followed by screams of pain, we figure they're good.) Those playdates eventually transform into dinner dates or ladies' nights. We enjoy each other's company for the togetherness, the validation, the support, the sharing, and the simple ease of conversation we wished we got from our men. Ha ha ha . . . kidding. Sort of.

And then the school year ends. The kids promise to see each other over the summer, to go swimming and to the park, and maybe to hit the zoo together a couple times. And it may even happen. But we, being adults, realize the truth for what it is.

We're breaking up.

It's a twist on the May–December romance, this friendship we have, except our relationship begins in September and ends in May. And, of course, doesn't involve jewelry.

It can't be helped; it's bad timing, is all. No one's to blame; no one did anything wrong. It's just that our kids are going to different schools in the fall, and they'll be moving on to new friends. This means we too will be moving on to new friends, because there are only a certain number of hours in a day and most moms just don't have time for their own friends without some kind of child-based justification.

So each year, on the last day of preschool, the kids run out of school, jumping for joy, and the moms kind of skulk out, heads down, glancing sideways at the friends they may or may not run into in the grocery store from now on.

"Well, I guess this is it," we'll say. "I had a good time. Take care. Good luck with little Billy's, uh, 'issue.' Call if I can help. Really. I mean it. Now give us a hug!"

This last, of course, is said through tears, tears that we try to hide with feeble excuses; "The sun's in my eyes," or "I just stepped on a piece of glass." We try to be brave, but we know what's going on. Our hearts are breaking. It's as simple and pathetic as that.

As I write this, another preschool year is coming to a close, and I've decided that I'm not going to let this happen again without saying how I feel.

So. To all the girls I've laughed with, cried with, and walked through muddy fieldtrips with: I had a good time. I really did. I already miss you. Maybe we can get together again sometime. Like when our kids graduate high school.

Love,

Maggie

collateral damage

BY JANE HODGES

ear J.,

At first I felt bad about not inviting you to my wedding last summer. But as time has passed, I've become more comfortable with that decision—and what the decision really concerns, which is this: After twenty years, we are no longer friends.

You bailed on me.

The last time I saw you? March 2006. We'd both flown from our separate cities to the Bay Area for a girls' weekend that dovetailed with a conference you attended. Harried and behind on work, we summoned our best procrastinator's denial and shucked our worries when we crossed the Golden Gate Bridge en route to the wine country. We listened to Beck and Neko Case and discussed our weekend—an orgy of spa appointments and wine-tastings and dinner reservations in Healdsburg and Calistoga and Napa. It's what we do when we're together: We drive to hedonistic activities, yakking the whole way about books and film and the DSM-IV classifications of our favorite celebrities, imbalanced authors, and mutual friends.

I can't think of anything I could have done to upset you. The only difference between this trip and roundups past was that this time, each night before bed, I called my boyfriend to say goodnight—just a brief call, nothing mushy. I knew you were concerned somehow about my relationship, but I didn't know the motive for or nature of your concern. When I told you Dave was going to sell his home and move in with me during the summer of 2006, you told me (projection alert!) that I didn't sound excited enough about it, as if you were helping me notice a flashing yellow light dangling above a dangerous intersection.

Of course, your comment supposes I *wanted* excitement in a relationship, when what I wanted was stability, comfort, someone to trust, a partner to share in plans and make me laugh. Most of the *excitement* I'd experienced in the dating space was really the anxiety of wondering whether I was in a relationship or just imagining the potential for one with some distracted guy. Excitement was *your* deal, because any kind of dating would have been exciting to you—if you'd let yourself do it.

For most of the time we've known one another, I've held love relationships in higher esteem than you have. Dating was always an important but impossible goal for me, something I knew I needed to do to grow as a person, something that I knew would be hard for me (crazy family, hello) but necessary.

But as you know, until 2004 the men I tried dating were like a rare species of bird that I briefly spotted and held on my arm before they sank their claws in to get lift-off, resuming their migration toward women who mattered more to them than I ever would.

They were lessons about my insignificance to the people whose approval I most wanted, tests of self-esteem I was no stranger to. Comments like *You know I don't love you* and *My therapist says I'm just sleeping with you to get back at my ex-wife* and, my personal favorite, *I haven't been very nice to you, and you haven't gotten upset enough about it—I really think you need to go to a therapist.*

But that didn't make me turn my back on relationships with men. It wasn't that I felt that relationships were impossible. They just weren't possible with the men I'd chosen thus far.

You've never dated since I've known you (and if you are now, I wish you luck), and the only fooling-around you've ever disclosed took place on a cruise vacation you took with your parents overseas, where the sun and grappa and some hot Italian guy you met made you relax your considerable defenses long enough to taste possibility. You're too good for the messy emotional scrum, the necessary Sturm und Drang. Yours wasn't an earned cynicism, a break you took after heartache. In your head, you'd decided that all dating was suspect, a time waster, a way women sabotage and distract themselves from self-sufficiency, creativity, accomplishment. For the most part, you laughed off dating during and after undergrad while noting the stupidity of frat boys, and you laughed it off in medical school while noting the ludicrousness of romance among med students. As our twenties advanced, you lamented some of our female college classmates' decisions to marry early and drop out of careers, letting their husbands bring home the dough while they wasted Dartmouth diplomas on Round 2 of girlhood (this time with a live baby doll!), knitting, tea time. On this last point, I agreed with your horror: We called such gals "throwbacks," and we mocked them mercilessly, considering them nothing more than thoroughbred breeders with expensive diplomas.

I don't know why I thought *my* arrival at the doorstep of a good relationship wouldn't bother you. I guess I felt like I'd worked through all the genres and forms of relationships and had learned from them, and that the big-R Relationship I'd found hadn't compromised me in any of the awful ways we'd seen mutual acquaintances lose themselves. I was no "throw-back." Besides, you always seemed amused by my dating stories, supportive but firm in your position as conscientious objector to the whole energy-sucking, insecurity-generating business of attempted couple-dom. You didn't judge my interest in finding love, sex, companionship, or some mix of the three. You just thought it was a funny affliction that I, an otherwise sensible woman, indulged. Maybe I never noticed that as long as I was failing at love, my investments in the acts surrounding it were okay with you. Like Sisyphus, I could push the rock up the hill, and as long as I never succeeded at moving it permanently, you could ignore that I was actually toughening up in essential ways. Perhaps my repeated poor results reinforced your position: The best romantic relationship is none.

The boyfriend I was seeing during our Bay Area trip was different, though, and you and I both knew it. He was solid and real. Somewhere between our Calistoga mud soak and the champagne we couldn't afford at Cyrus, I told you a little detail about my relationship with him that should've tipped me off to your low tolerance for my arrival at love. I told you about a stupid falsetto voice I'd invented to goad him and a stupid ticklish punishment he'd concocted in return. I wanted you to know that things with him were good, to know a little more about him: that he is silly and funny like we were, that he is one of us, that nothing is changing dramatically.

But you recoiled in teenage horror.

"Oh my God, dude," you said. "You're totally going to marry him!"

You weren't exclamatory in an excited way, but rather an accusatory, suspicious one. It was as if I had committed some giant personal gaffe—slept with a married man, shoplifted, walked around New York City oblivious to a spot of menstrual blood on the back of my white skirt. There was palpable danger in your voice. Of course, major movement in life always necessitates danger, and I thought you were apprehending that, at thirty-six, I was on the cusp of a major choice and change—which I was; after all, this was the first man to move in—and that you were on my side, even if you had to digest the news a little. I didn't understand that the danger I sensed was our friendship's fragility, and that somewhere inside of you, a tide was receding, rolling out permanently to the horizon where you prefer to live, insulated from the dangerous business of clanging bodies or day-to-day partnership.

There were a few strange moments on the trip. You got angry about a flight delay on JetBlue, the airline I'd recommended to you. I got angry about a snafu I'd made in scheduling one of our very expensive spa procedures. But at some point you remarked that we'd been friends for sixteen years, and while that made me happy, it's also true in my experience that such comments only surface when the relationship in question has hit a tipping point.

I remember a boyfriend whose housemate told me *I think you're really good for him.* I wanted to enjoy the compliment, but I couldn't. I didn't want to be "good for" someone, like a vitamin. I wanted us to be good *together.* He broke up with me within weeks, just like you would. But at least he had the balls to announce the news, cornering me with it at the NoHo Star bar minutes before friends came to meet us.

After our spa weekend, I went back to Seattle and helped my man refurbish and sell his house and move in with me. You went back to New York and resumed your teaching and private practice and the occasional moonlighting job, and your world of med school friends and artsy interests. We swapped a few emails, and then in September 2006, you wrote back briefly that you were *really swamped.* This was fairly commonplace, so I thought nothing of it.

But then began the silence.

For the first two years after you stopped responding to calls and emails, I worried about you and your workload, and the pressure you put on yourself, and your student loan debt from medical school, and whether it's healthy for you to work so hard to please your supervisor, who seems to expect a lot of you. I realized, maybe too late, it might be weird for you that I was in a serious relationship and that you might be uncomfortable about it, and I questioned what might be going on for you—if you needed empathy and understanding, what insensitivity I might have presented to spur your silence, or what depression or sadness or overwhelming self-loathing had turned you inward and away from people you'd known a long time. I sent you emails

and left you voicemails periodically—pretending I wasn't as upset and worried and hurt as I was, and hoping I wouldn't seem
like a stalker—and I asked you over voicemail, finally, if I'd done
anything to upset or offend you or if you were just really busy.
But I never heard back. You offered nothing but a bitchy, punishing silence.

My life moved on, but I didn't know what to do with your
silence. It was striking to me that you vanished from my life in
the moment when some aspects of it solidified—and solidified
positively. Rejection accompanying success rankled me in a familiar way—in fact, a family-familiar way—but I never expected it from you, the first friend whose flowers arrived when my
mother died, the pal who got me laughing again when I lived on
entry-level publishing salaries and bounced rent checks. I was
there for you too, when you had health issues, when your mother had breast cancer, when you were broke in Boston and let me
send you a thick winter coat I never wore in Seattle.

But as I began planning my wedding, thinking about a pas-
sage in my life and who I wanted around me—who is there for
me and why, who isn't and why—I stepped back and asked a
different question about you and your disappearance. I stopped
questioning why you had stopped talking to me and what I
might have done to cause that, and I began asking myself why
I cared.

You take issue with the concept of human need. You're unable to fathom people relying on one another, because you aren't
comfortable receiving attention—only giving it. Your rejection
wasn't just of me but of a reality in my life that offends your
sensibilities.

Why, really, did I want to be in touch? What would happen if you never returned my calls? You hadn't exactly been supportive of my relationship, and you were the lone dissenter among my friends. Did I really expect you'd come and celebrate with me, considering your years of silence, considering the fact you couldn't even tell me what was going on with your life, your happiness or your problems?

I catalogued all the reasons I missed you, but they kept rooting and situating themselves in the deep past, in sentimentality and habit. When I love people, I see their best qualities. But ours, alas, was a case of "misery loves company." We always shored each other up when we were unhappy. I guess as our lives improved—as mine did, anyway—there was less to discuss.

We met during a college semester abroad in France, two lonely baffled people somewhat embarrassed at our disappointment with the extrovert-oriented social life at Dartmouth, and we became thick friends thereafter. We loved literature, psychology, drama, and amusing ourselves while bullshitting our way through Literature and Psychoanalysis, a class taught by a fat, knighted French scholar who resembled Flaubert and wound up with spittle in his beard during impassioned discourses on Lacan and Foucault, Derrida and "The Dora Case."

We bonded over our wounds—similarly crazy families, in which our flaky fathers had lost lots of money, our mothers were angry yet too cowardly to divorce, our siblings were needy and spoiled, and we were the competent ones expected to problem-solve and coddle everyone else and sail through unscathed. We'd had unconventional childhoods, and we were judgmental and silently angry and psychologically astute from years of shouldering burdens belonging to other people.

We compared ourselves to Statler and Waldorf, the wry judges from *The Muppet Show* who didn't participate in the drama but instead sat back, commenting on it and judging it. We disliked the same sorts of people for the same sorts of reasons. But eventually, I wanted to participate in life's mess and see what happened. I think you preferred your balcony seat, covering over your discomforts with a busy schedule and too many obligations for your own good, the simplicity of a platonic relationship between you and a boss/mentor.

After college we never lived in the same city except once—1998, the year you did a residency in New York and had a health problem that temporarily messed up your hormones and, you claimed, your hair. You thought it was falling out and visibly thinner and you were becoming a monster. As a Leo, you were very self-conscious about it and refused to believe my protests that your hair looked fine, truly. I suppose I wasn't much cheer, because I was having a pretty good year, all things considered. I had a fancy job, less fiscal worry, travel assignments.

One day during this time, you were unusually curt with me on the phone, so I called back and asked if you were upset, and, if you were, whether I had done anything to provoke that. Frankly, you were rude, which I didn't say, but I wanted to make sure I hadn't done something wrong. You had never taken that tone with me before.

"Everything isn't about you," you said, seething, manipulating my intent.

I had asked if you were upset, which you couldn't answer. I had asked if I had impacted you and needed to apologize, and you couldn't answer. You just told me you were self-absorbed with your own misery, and that it was *your* misery, your precious, precious, misery.

I waited for you to contact me after that, happy for a break if you were going to sulk. Finally, after several months, you called up and said, *Hey dude, you probably think I'm crazy.* But I didn't, and our friendship resumed. You went on to graduate med school, finished a fellowship, and began practicing psychiatry. I went on to work as a freelance writer, to hire a therapist and move across the country to a city that's less stressful for me, to buy a home and embark on a series of relationships that ended with a good one.

I guess the clues were always there. Ours was a friendship of youthful angst, one where the secret contract required mutual unhappiness—and you'd upheld the unhappiness part of the bargain, while I, perhaps, abandoned it. So wanting to invite you to my wedding, to carry your friendship forward was, woefully, a waste. But even so, I regret that this is where you are—if I'm even right about any of it. Minus any contact, I can only guess. I realized inviting you to my wedding would only provide you with another opportunity to withhold a reply, and so this time I didn't reach out, but instead protected myself.

Even after I made the decision, though, I felt bad about it. I wanted to find a way for us to be friends, but you'd have to want to participate in that. I can't lower myself to your emotional level to make you feel more comfortable when you're the person who resents my having a relationship because you're too cowardly to try one.

Last summer, about six weeks before my wedding, I had a dream: I was sitting at a big banquet table sharing a meal with friends from many parts of my life, and you were sitting on the end of that table, to my right side—the side closest to my right brain, I guess.

"Why did you stop returning my calls and emails?" I asked, queasy for an answer.

"It's because, oh, I don't know, I've just been really busy," you said, trailing off, looking away, like that was sufficient.

Even in my dream, I wasn't satisfied with that answer. Here I was screwing up the courage to ask how you felt, in order to understand what had happened, and you couldn't even do me the favor of a response. I tapped you on the shoulder to tell you so.

"I don't think that's why you stopped calling," I said. "I think it's because you're a cunt."

Consciously, that's not how I regard you. I feel sorry for you, feel sorry that you would judge me or eliminate me from your life because I chose to share my life with a man, feel sorry that you think your life is full of inevitable difficulties when you've made deliberate choices that keep it difficult at every turn, feel sorry that you've chosen to martyr yourself according to some overachieving Good Girl narrative that works for you, makes your bosses and parents happy, and makes you run from any peers who make themselves happy. You don't owe me an apology. You owe yourself one.

Yours sincerely,

Jane

a voice from the future
BY GABRIELLE STUDENMUND

ear Gabby,

I'm writing to you from your future. And I have some bad news for you. It has to do with your obsession with fitness. It's dangerous.

Don't you already know that you are fast and strong? Didn't you feel that way while training for and running two marathons? Do you really have to push yourself even more by taking on a half-Ironman triathlon?

I know, I know. You are a talented swimmer—your team even won high school state championships. And combined with your new love of running marathons, a triathlon may *appear* to be the right thing to do. Yes, your dear boyfriend Wayne has indulged your fitness fantasies by giving you a Trek bicycle, just like the one your hero, Lance Armstrong, rides for his Tour de France championships.

But you need to ignore those signs that suggest your next race should be a triathlon. Think about it. You finally got what you've wanted for all these years: a position as senior editor at a national magazine. Do not push yourself further just because you think it will yield the physique of your dreams and make for a great article to the loyal readers of *Self*.

You need to resist the temptations to live your job, to seek überfitness. Instead, can I suggest slowing down a little? Why don't you just learn to enjoy the fruits of your labor of the last ten years, starting with your editorship of the University of Wyoming's student newspaper and leading you to the magazine-publishing world in Manhattan? Go out and celebrate your three-year anniversary with your gorgeous blind-date-turned-live-in boyfriend, Wayne. Enjoy a relaxing dinner with him instead of stressing out about having to get up early to cycle with your dear friends Laurel, Ramon, Alyssa, and Crispy.

I mean, don't you remember your first bike wreck? Don't you remember when your sister Maya unhooked the brakes to her bike to prevent you from borrowing it? How you rode down that hill in Lander, Wyoming, and had to bail when you realized the brakes were not working? You should have learned then to stay away from bicycles.

Because here's what happens. The day after your anniversary with Wayne, you get up early in the morning. You go to meet your friends for a bike ride. And you have a devastating accident. One that will end your life as a prominent magazine editor. One that will end your relationship with Wayne. One that will erase a year or so of your memories. One that will give you permanent brain injury. One that will force you to leave the city you love and have succeeded in.

It's an accident that will end your life as you know it, and that will nearly end your life altogether. You will lie in a coma for ten days with a breathing tube that leaves a lifelong scar. You will shatter your left elbow. Your metabolism will be ruined.

You, a marathon runner, will have to learn how to walk all over again. It will take you months to learn how to balance without pulling down your mother, who's always there for you, a human crutch if you will. Now, instead of running through Central Park, you walk around Southern Pines, a small Southern town near your family. And you tire after doing a few errands and need to go home to rest on your comfortable couch, mimicking your lazy cat Lucy (and by the way, you do walk everywhere—you can't drive, because your reaction times are too slow). And forget about wearing the perfect size 6 anymore. In your Southern life you will put on an extra twenty-five pounds that you will hate and will always struggle with, doubling you to a size 12.

Your brain damage leaves you with an inability to concentrate. When you call someone, you hope to remember who it is you're calling by the time they answer the phone. You'll become a slave to your calendars, planners, and lists, because without them, you'd be lost, and you have anxiety about losing your well-kept grocery list, because you'd have no idea what to get without that written idea of ingredients you need.

It's not that life is so terrible, don't get me wrong. It takes a while, but eventually, you find the right man and start writing again (though you still have that bad habit of typing with one hand, thanks to what you've done to your left elbow, which makes it hard for you to move your entire arm). You eventually learn your way around Southern Pines. After several years of therapies (physical, cognitive, occupational, speech), you do, eventually, become the independent woman you once were. You fall in love with your small town, and you are happy with your writing assignments for the local magazine *Pinestraw*. You are near and dear to your family members, who live close by and visit often. But sorry, Gabby. You're going to have to say goodbye to academic achievements, to buying whatever you please, to getting published monthly and being read by millions. Jumping on that bike puts an end to everything you've worked so hard to achieve.

What I wouldn't do to be able to actually send you this letter. To make sure you receive it. To warn you. To change the past. To prevent you from getting on that bike.

Gabby, can you hear me?

Your friend,

Gabrielle

i'm not you, but
i play you on the internet:
a letter to sarah palin

BY SARA BENINCASA

ear Sarah Palin:

Hi.

That seems like a fair enough place to start.

You're a fortysomething failed sports reporter/beauty-pageant contestant who recently made it to the top of Alaska politics and *almost* grabbed a really big Federal gig.

I'm a twentysomething failed schoolteacher/former beauty-pageant contestant who recently made it to the top of the stairs of my apartment building and *almost* got inside before puking everywhere (dinner was rough, heavy on the shellfish).

Okay, so our victories are different, and yours are surely larger than mine, but I like to think they connect us somehow.

I must clarify something about my beauty pageant experience. I was in seventh grade, a girl who grew up behind thick glasses under a mound of unruly hair. I had just gotten contact lenses and felt pretty for the first time in my entire life. I took up baton twirling, a gateway activity that frequently leads to entrance into the sordid underworld of tweenage beauty pageants. The conclusion of my short career in pageants was this: I placed 86th out of 88 girls at the 1994 Miss Majorette of America (Novice Division, 12- to 15-Year-Olds) competition in South Bend, Indiana. It was a stinging defeat.

Which leads me to another thing we have in common: the painful experience of being rejected for a job we *know* we were born to do.

I would have made a great 1994 Miss Majorette of America (Novice Division, 12- to 15-Year-Olds). I would have smiled and waved and worn big poofy dresses and sported big hair and gone on to the 1995 Miss Majorette of America competition to crown my lucky successor.

And you, Sarah, would have made a great vice president of the United States. You would have smiled and waved and worn big poofy dresses and sported big hair and gone on to the 2012 Republican National Convention to punch out anyone who attempted to become your successor. Then, after a glorious reelection and four more fun years as VP, you would have gone to the 2016 RNC to actually set ablaze anyone who tried to keep you from your rightful spot as Republican presidential nominee. In January of 2017, you would have smiled warmly and happily at the crowds of protesters gathered to egg your motorcade as you proceeded to the Capitol for your presidential inauguration that seemed like a ridiculous nightmare only a few years before—a ridiculous nightmare to everyone but *you*, Sarah.

And here we come to the most important difference between you and I, Sarah: *your* dream job could still become a reality! Not in the way described above, of course—not in the way you envisioned it the moment John McCain officially lost his shot at the presidency by picking up the phone and giving you a very special ring-a-ding. No, Sarah, your shot at the Oval Office simply requires a series of unfortunate first-term fuckups by our current president, who has been tasked with the easy job of:

making the economy perfect, restoring America's image as a beacon of hope and freedom, finishing up the catastrophic war that has slaughtered tens of thousands of innocent women and children in Iraq, establishing peace between the murderous imbeciles in Jerusalem and the murderous imbeciles who hate them, cleaning up the oceans, making the big hole in the sky go away, making the homosexuals think he loves them, making the heterosexuals who don't love homosexuals think he loves them, ending racism forever, and making abortion unnecessary in a world where contraception never fails, unwanted pregnancy never happens, and children are always loved.

If he fails to do any one of those things, lots of people are going to say that he doesn't deserve a second shot at the presidency. If he fails to do all of those things, lots *more* people are going to say that he doesn't have a snowball's chance in hell of getting reelected.

And if there's any political player on the national scene who represents the absolute *opposite* of Barack Obama and the characteristics he attempts to embody (dignity, grace, sophistication, intellectualism, multiculturalism), it's you, Sarah. Your particular brand of genius is that you appeal to the worst of America: Our wholesale rejection of book learnin'; our proud disinterest in affairs unrelated to sports, reality television, and guns; and our fondness for people who reproduce at an irresponsible and mildly disturbing rate. (See: the Duggar family and "Jon and Kate Plus Eight." And if the Octomom had a nice husband and a pretty house, she'd be an American heroine instead of a despised freak.)

My big-city liberal friends say you're finished, but I know that's wishful thinking on their parts—and a bit naive too, if you ask me. Having lived in suburban New Mexico, rural North Carolina, and rural New Jersey (yes, it exists), I can attest to the fact that there are plenty of people who've wanted to elect someone like you for years—and they haven't given up just because that elitist Mohammedan Black Panther got himself voted into office.

So I'm here to tell you that I know you've got a real shot in 2012.

Sure, I'm a liberal; sure, I advocate for real sex education for children and teens; sure, I think abortion should be safe, legal, affordable, and widely available to teens and adults. I'm not saying I'm going to *vote* for you, Sarah. But I am saying that a lot of people would love to do so, and their numbers will only grow if Barack Obama fails to live up to the Black Jesus unicorn-magic standards we've all set for him.

Oh, and there's one more very important reason you've got a shot in 2012: Real Americans *love* a comeback kid.

And Jesus.

But then again, isn't Jesus the ultimate comeback kid, if you think about it?

Yours,

Sara Benincasa

at-home mothers need not apply

BY N. AHERN

ear Marnie,

You probably don't remember the day you made me feel like a farm animal instead of a professional. And if you do remember, it's the sort of thing that would make you furrow your perfectly waxed eyebrows, hold your hands palm-up (if they weren't busy with the Blackberry), and say, "What was the big deal?"

I'm usually a What's the Big Deal kind of person too. All kinds of things roll off my back. They had to; after all, our grad school was not the kind of place that suffered fools or indulged hurt feelings. But the fact that this still bothers me tells me it probably isn't going away.

When you were launching your working women's networking club six or seven years ago, I was happy for you. You worked hard, doing it on the side of a full-time job and with two young kids, and when you asked for help spreading the word, I didn't mind. Yes, I had two young kids and was working too, but I was self-employed and working from home, and my contracts were flexible. The club was a great idea, with hot lecture topics and the chance to network with an A-list of members in town. I would have liked to join, but we were about to move to the West Coast for Steve's job.

Over the next few years, the club really took off, apparently. Lectures and social events were standing room only, with women from all kinds of professional fields in town. You were written up in the paper as a mobilizer, one of the city's top entrepreneurs to watch. When we moved back three years later, I was looking forward to joining. My work had gone down to part-time since having my fourth child, and I saw it as a great way to get plugged back into the city and keep a foot in the working world.

But when I mentioned it to you, you squirmed. You said something to the effect of "I'll see what I can do," but that new members had to be approved by committee and were limited to a certain number a year.

It was so obvious what was going on that we both had to pretend it wasn't. You didn't bring it up again, and neither did I.

If I were a different kind of person, I'd have called you on it right there: "Oh that's bull, of course you can get me in, you *own* the damn thing." Or maybe if I were more of a toot-my-own-horn kind of person, I would have started talking more about the work I'm doing. I could have started making baldly self-aggrandizing references to clients and projects, even if they were fewer and further between than they once were, could have done some name-dropping about the television appearances I'd done in the not-*too*-too-distant past, could have made sure you knew

I was still on the board of my old company. But that's not my style, and anyway, I'm too proud to force my way in somewhere I'm not wanted.

Since your breakup, you've been wanting to get together more often—pep talks over drinks, activities to buoy your spirits. "You're so grounded," you tell me. "You're so *healthy* that you've never even been in *therapy*."

The irony here is rich but stings: You value my stability but think being grounded is the opposite of being a hip professional.

You might also take note, while we're out for the night, that it's actually possible for a mother of four to get out of the house. Steve watches the kids, or I get a sitter, just like I do occasionally for professional events. Just like I would have done to go to your club meetings.

I already know what you'd say: That the club really has a quota and an approval process, it's gotten so big, yadda yadda yadda. But you could have started up the machinery for me if you wanted me in. And you don't, so you didn't. It's that simple.

If there was any doubt about the way you perceive my professionalism, now that I'm primarily at home with the kids, it's gone now. The look on your face last week when you saw that I was pregnant with Number Five was really something, like I was part Jersey cow. I really think there's a part of you that believes women are less interesting when they spend too much time with their children. Were you afraid I'd embarrass you at the club by talking about epidurals and breastfeeding instead of investment strategies? Do you think I checked my brain at the door the last time I was discharged from the Labor & Delivery ward? There are people I expect this sort of thinking from—

some of my PTO friends' husbands, some of my husband's colleagues, even some of my clients. Whenever we move, I still print up business cards for this reason: Because there are some people who won't respect your input unless you have a title in a glitzy font. But I wouldn't have expected a fellow working mother and friend to be one of them.

Next time we're at some liberal fundraiser and you get talking about prejudice and stereotypes, pardon me if I choke and spill my cranberry-and-soda down my maternity dress. But I won't make a big deal about the hypocrisy. Because I'm too healthy and grounded for that.

Cheers,

Me

on exes and thin mints

BY MARGARET LITTMAN

ear Kath,

If I were in Hollywood, I'd be sitting at a typewriter with the stereotypical trash can overflowing with crumpled drafts, the balled-up papers dotting my office floor. My literal and metaphoric missed shots laid out around me. That's how many times I have started this letter to you.

But I'm not a scriptwriter, and this is still my awkward real life. So I'm doing yet another Select All, Delete, on the laptop and trying again.

After all these years and all the ways in which our lives have intersected, we still don't know each other that well. But I have always tried to be sympathetic to your point of view, even if I could not be empathetic. I know it must be weird to have your new-boyfriend-then-fiancé-then-husband-then-father-of-your-child be best friends with his ex. Particularly when your first husband cheated on you. While you had a newborn. I know that

you've witnessed people justifying their very bad behavior because they were "following their heart," as if that is a Get Out of
Jail Free card that excuses everything. I am thankful to have never
been in that situation. I appreciate that I will never appreciate
how an experience like that breeds mistrust.

And I appreciate the school of thought that says you keep
your husband away from exes for the same reason you don't
keep Girl Scout cookies in the house while you're dieting. No
need to fight temptation.

But Thor isn't your ex, and I'm not a temptress. Thor and I
lived together for seven years because we liked each other. We
broke up because we weren't good as a couple. If we wanted to
be together, we would be. We could be. We decided not to be.
After we broke up ten years ago, we chose to work through any
awkwardness or jealousy about each other's new relationships
because it was so important to us to stay friends. Neither of us
could imagine a life without the other.

I can't exactly explain our friendship, except to say we get
each other. We get the people we used to be. And we like getting
to know the people we are becoming.

We have similar senses of humor. And work ethics. And
senses of loyalty.

Nine years ago, when you and Thor first dated, I thought
maybe you and I would eventually become friendly. We were
not ever going to be girlfriends who go to the mall together.
We're not those kinds of girls. And we already have those kinds
of friends. We're not going to vacation together with our new
partners in Cancún, or even double-date at the movies. But I
did think you and your kids would someday be at the table of

one of my huge Passover seders. And I did think we'd at least have pleasant conversation if you answered the phone when I called Thor.

I've tried hard to be the kind of friend (to Thor, if not to you) that you need me to be, letting him take the initiative in how much we see each other or talk to each other. When you announced your engagement five years ago, I spent months thinking of a wedding gift that I thought you would love and use, and something your whole family could enjoy—not just something I knew Thor wanted on his own. Last year I did the same when selecting a baby gift that included your entire blended family.

I wish you could be a fly on the wall during a conversation between Thor and me, because then you'd get it. Then you'd understand that when we talk, it is about innocuous things. Work and politics and how to get rid of moles in our yards and your family. We talk about your kids. How when your baby, Stephen, smiles, Thor just wants to watch him all day, even if there is baseball on TV or a deadline looming. Or about the running jokes he and Alexa, your daughter from your first marriage, have, and how happy it made him when she gave him his first Father's Day card.

For a while I didn't realize you were uncomfortable with our being friends. When we'd go our separate ways after dinner, I'd say, "Say hi to Kath." Or, "Tell Kath I'm sorry she couldn't make it." His face would fall just enough for me to do a double take. But I never asked him about it.

Then, one Tuesday last year, he emailed asking if I had seen *How I Met Your Mother* the night before. It was the episode where Ted tries to do the right thing and invites his fiancée's ex (and the father of her child) to their wedding. The ex shows up, and in the end, Ted gets left at the altar. The Hollywood message: Never invite an ex to your wedding.

I had already been to your wedding. I danced at your wedding. I drank at your wedding, true, but not so much that there was a scene, and I walked home unassisted. No Hollywood drama.

But that's when I knew that still, almost a decade since Thor and I split (longer than the time we were together), you were not okay with this friendship. So I offered to fade into the past, if that would make it easier, because your family is more important than our friendship.

But here's the thing: I don't believe that Thor should have to make those kinds of sacrifices for marriage. I think a marriage should expand your network of friends and loved ones, not shrink it.

I don't know if Thor told you, but the guy I was dating recently broke up with me out of the blue. He reconnected with his ex, "the one who got away," and they wanted to give it another try. I guess that was my little cosmic exercise in empathy. Or irony. I told Thor when it was still raw and I was still sad, because he is my best friend. Because he knows when to be a shoulder to cry on and when to call me on my bullshit. That's why I'm friends with him, although the word "friend" sounds hollow. He is my BFF, my other brother, my former editor and sounding board. He taught me to play cribbage, bet the trifecta, refinish furniture, and to never split fives in Blackjack. He is the keeper of my inside jokes, and the ashes of the dogs we owned together.

The thing he is not, and will never be again: my lover.

Despite my experiences, I still firmly believe that you shouldn't ban an ex. Because here's the thing: Even if you prohibit someone from seeing his ex, one day they'll run into each other at the grocery store. And either they'll realize they made a mistake, like an episode of *How I Met Your Mother,* or they won't. And whether they've talked every week for the last decade or didn't even know which state each other lived in, it makes no difference. Because either you are the kind of person who leaves your relationship for your ex or you aren't.

So this is my plea. Please don't stop us from seeing each other. Not for my sake, but for his. And for yours. His devotion to you and your family is complete and pure. To know that you don't trust him because of what other people have done, or because of what Hollywood would say, would kill a little part of his soul. You deserve to have him with his soul intact.

Plus, I know how skinny you are, even postpartum and post-forty. You can stand to have a cookie in the house.

Best,

Margaret

you don't know me, but you changed my life

BY MARY EMERICK

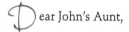ear John's Aunt,

You don't know me. I doubt you even remember the wide-eyed girl hanging on your words that summer night back in 1985. So it is a bit presumptuous of me to call you my friend. It's just that you have been with me for the past twenty-five years. You have never left me, unlike other summertime friends, who faded away into the distance. You never judged me like some have, no matter how deep the mistakes I have made. I have leaned on you during the times when the mountain seemed too tough to climb, the snow too deep, the pain too intense. You have been that voice inside my head that told me I could get up off the floor and go on. You have been the one I have followed and never could quite catch.

Let me explain. It all began when I met you that crazy, lilac-scented summer when your nephew John and I were college students working on Mackinac Island in northern Michigan. He and

I lived in the Mission House, an ancient dormitory that we swore was haunted by its former residents. The long white porch was where we spent most of our evenings, watching the sun set over Lake Huron, making up stories about where we had been and where we wanted to go. Strangers, friends, and relatives came and went—it was a shifting, colorful group.

You came to visit, stopping over on the way to your next adventure. I can still envision you, your pale hair in a braid, your eyes blazing, fresh off a monthlong sailing trip to Tasmania. I was twenty at the time, and you must have been at least one and a half times that. You had jumped aboard the boat on a whim, knowing nobody, answering a "crew wanted" ad posted someplace in San Diego. You did not think it over, agonize, wonder what people would think. You just went for it. And I admired you for it.

You see, before I met you, I thought my life was on a clean, safe trajectory. Go to college. Get a job in an office. Marry someone from the air force base. That summer, I was grasping the last freedom I thought I would ever have before my life became ordinary.

After you kissed John on the cheek and left for the night, I spent a sleepless night in my single bed. I never saw you after that night, but that was when I decided I wanted to be like you. I wanted to have an adventurous life, walk without a net. I wanted to break out of the boundaries that were defined for girls like me. For the first time, I understood that I could. You showed me that women can do more, that our skies are limitless too.

Because of you, I got a job fighting wildfires from Florida to Alaska with a group of men who didn't believe I could keep up on the hikes or carry the loads. Because of you, I showed them that a woman can be both tough and beautiful. Because of you, I backpacked alone along the spine of the Rockies and paddled a kayak in twelve-foot seas along Alaska's coast. Because of you, I dusted myself off after each tumble and kept climbing upward.

It has been a rollercoaster ride to say the least. I've lived in more states than I can remember. I have loved a smokejumper, a hunter, a sweet-eyed boy on a bike. Some of them loved me back. I have been lost in the wilderness; I've had to run to escape a fire. But I have also woken up on the granite belly of a mountain, watching bighorn sheep come down to a lake to drink. I've paddled a slim yellow kayak a few feet offshore a tidal estuary, watching bears come out of the forest like shadows.

If I could talk to you now, I would ask you if it was all worth it in the end. I wonder if you would have cashed it in for security, and for the same bed every night. For me, there were men who wanted to stay home, to push lawnmowers and have children. There were people who lay awake at night wondering where I was and if I was safe. There was a marriage that did not last. I take the blame and burden for all of these. I wonder if you feel the same dilemma—the seduction of a safe harbor but the call of the wind and the waves.

I have tried to find you over the years, but I don't even remember John's last name or where he went. All of us from that summer have scattered, leaving no trace. The last time I was on that island, the college students on the Mission House porch looked so young, their faces fresh and open as flowers. I felt like you must have when you came, no common ground to meet upon. It is true after all: You can never really go back.

So we go on. I've never really known if I was making the right choices. Like the fishermen out in Sitka Sound, I cast my net wide and see what I catch. I leap off cliffs, trusting that the landing will be soft. I fly in small planes. I dare to love again.

And I think of you often. You must be in your late fifties now, maybe older. I could pass you on the street and never recognize your face. You might even be the woman I see on my street in Alaska, her long white hair flying like a banner as she rides her bike down to the harbor and her kayak.

If you have slowed down, given in, I don't really want to know. I hope you are still out there clamping on to every opportunity. I don't really want to catch up with you, though. I prefer to think of you just slightly ahead of me, showing me the way.

Sincerely,

Mary

the lost language of lox

BY LORI HORVITZ

ear Cheryl,

We met in a fiction-writing workshop in September of 1997, both of us doctoral students at SUNY Albany. You wrote stories about drunken escapades: one that took place on a Pepto-Bismol-colored bus in Nantucket; another about a marine who lured the narrator into his pickup truck and tried to pull off her shirt, but she ran, leaving one of her sneakers in his possession. Soon I learned there was nothing fictional about your stories.

Once the class ended, we bumped into each other in the university parking lot. "Let's drink whiskey together," you said. "Sounds like fun," I said, thinking *How sweet. A young, cute, all-American blond girl wanting to be my friend*. Even though you were a devout Christian, you wore a Star of David around your neck. I asked you why and you said you believed in the Jewish roots of Christianity. And that you loved Jewish people.

We began to talk on a daily basis. You told me about your boyfriend of five years who studied marine biology in Indiana and wanted to marry you. You said, "Maybe I'm in love with him but I just don't know it. I rarely see him and only call him when I'm drunk."

At last, I spoke openly about my sexuality instead of hiding it. I told you about my relationship with my last girlfriend, a Mexican scientist who studied in New York for two years before returning to her country. In response, you said you'd never been with a woman but had had crushes on women, and added, "Any woman who says she hasn't thought about it is a big fat liar. Oh my gosh! I'm not hitting on you."

I didn't think of you as girlfriend material. You had a boy-friend. And you liked to drink. A lot. Besides, you were a practic-ing Christian, and I was a lapsed Jew.

When we met for Sunday brunch, we both ordered bagels and lox and spent the morning talking about the connections be-tween lox and love.

"It's pink and soft, like a heart," I said. "And they're almost spelled the same."

The next day, you emailed me:

oh my goodness . . . another similarity between love and lox¿
if you write loxloxloxloxloxloxloxloxloxloxlox, it looks like x's
and o's. I haven't figured out what the "l" would be all about,
though. Maybe it's like the number 1, so it could mean "one
hug kiss one hug kiss," and all the ones would add up to lots,
which are sometimes involved in love. I like that.

lox
Cheryl

A week later we took a day trip to Williamstown, Massachu-setts. I loved driving in the car with you, listening to the mixes you made for me, both of us singing at the top of our lungs to Joni Mitchell, Cat Stevens, the Indigo Girls. For a good part of our visit, because it was raining, we sat in a café/photolab.

"What a great idea," you said. "You can drink coffee while waiting for your pictures!"

I loved your optimism, your enthusiasm about everything, even a simple café. At the time, I had no idea about your ongoing depression. In fact, your cheerful disguise was so effective that a depressed classmate pulled you aside one day and said, "You give me so much hope. You're the happiest person I've ever met."

Two months into our friendship, my feelings about you shifted. *Did I like you? Did you like me? What about your boyfriend?* We spent more and more time together—sober time—playing guitar and singing, sharing our writing.

Since I didn't own a television, you brought your TV to my apartment. We watched Barbara Walters interview Ellen DeGeneres the week before Ellen came out on her own show. We slouched on my futon sofa, our legs stretched out on a milk crate, both of us drinking water.

"Water is so good!" you said. "What a great idea!"

After filling your water glass for a third time, I sat at least a foot away from you, making sure not to get too close. But when the show ended, you slumped your body toward mine. I moved away. You moved closer, and this time I couldn't help but lean over and kiss you. For the next hour, without saying a word, we kissed and held each other.

Before you left that night, I asked you what was going on.

With a nineteen-inch TV in your arms, you said, "Whatever it is, it feels good."

That night I had a dream about an orange stray cat. The tiny stray had a drippy, gray, almost glued-shut eye, but when I bent down to pet the cat, its eye fell out and transformed into an iridescent sphere of bright reds and blues and yellows, like a beautiful glass marble. I wondered if the cat represented you. Was I taking in a stray?

Together we spent time reciting poetry and plays, talking about writing and feminist theory, playing Scrabble. You offered insightful feedback about my writing and asked to see everything I'd written. Sometimes we'd write together and read aloud what we'd written and, always, you inspired me.

Three weeks into our relationship, at a martini party, you stumbled from one person to the next, telling each person you loved them. After six months, I noticed a trend; at parties, you drank and drank and drank until you sat in a corner and cried. So when a group of friends planned a party at a century-old house in the country—a sleepover party, a place I'd never been—I was hesitant to go. But we went, and you drank and drank, and when you ran out of cigarettes, you insisted I drive you to get more. When I refused, you cursed at me and ran out to the road.

"If you're not going to take me to get cigarettes," you wailed, "I'm going to hitchhike."

I chased after you, but you got to the road first and stuck out your thumb, just in time for a white Mack truck to stop. The door swung open. You lurched into the passenger seat, but before you had the chance to close the door, I ran up to the rig and pleaded with the driver not to take you. The engine vroomed and idled, and the mustached man in a green plaid flannel shirt eyed you, then me. You attempted to pull the door shut, but the truck driver leaned over and pushed it all the way open.

"Go back to your friend," he said. "I ain't taking you nowhere."

You ran out of the truck, back to the house. I thanked the driver. He could have raped you, cut your body into a thousand pieces, gagged and drowned you. But he let you go. He let you go back to the old house where you sat in a corner and cried. When I sat next to you, you laid your head in my lap. You wept, shook, apologized. I stroked your hair, calmed your trembling body.

And I wondered why I stayed with you. Was it the language we had developed together? Our playful conversations full of non sequiturs, starting with, let's say, lox and lint, shoes and schnauzers, moving onto eggplant and Toyotas, and ending with dolphin squeals in Brooklyn?

And after sleepless nights of my obsessing about my dead mother decomposing somewhere in New Jersey, you always held me, told me that everything was going to be okay.

"Your mother is so proud of you," you once said. And when you smiled, the right corner of your mouth slid up toward your cheekbone and took up half your face.

According to your Evangelical Christian parents, you were in the grips of Satan for loving another woman. How could this love that brought you so much happiness be the same love that caused you so much pain and guilt?

Now you drank at least a six-pack every night. When you were good and drunk, you called Take-Out Taxi, a food delivery service, and binged on chicken wings dipped in blue cheese,

cheese fries, ice cream. Once a slender athlete, a rower for your college crew team, now you were a round-faced chubby girl. You hated yourself.

Your guilt reminded me of my own feelings of inadequacy, of going to family events with cousins, their kids doing the hora, my ninety-seven-year-old grandmother asking if I'd met a special man, my father trying to set me up with a police sergeant. "He's Jewish," he said.

On the nights we didn't spend together, I wouldn't hear from you until two or three in the afternoon, when you woke up. Until you called, I worried you were covered by a morgue sheet. At your apartment, I couldn't ignore the dishes piled high in your sink, floating in vomit. I rinsed the dishes, swept the dust bunnies out of the corners of your room.

As I saw your alcohol dependency worsen, you rarely made it to your job on time, if at all. You couldn't stop bingeing on food. I did what I could: I offered to go to AA with you. During a therapy session, I pleaded with your therapist to do something. "If Cheryl continues like this," I said, "she'll be dead within the year."

Two years into our relationship, I accepted a full-time professorship in North Carolina. I wasn't sure how you would fit into my new life. After all, you were still in school. You were still drinking. At this point, you couldn't go a day without alcohol. In fact, on some nights, you'd swig down a twelve-pack of Budweiser, no problem.

The night before I left for North Carolina, you drank six beers, one after the next. On your couch, you plopped yourself down, apologized, and passed out. I pulled your sneakers off, put a blanket over your body, a plastic bucket by your head. I sighed, glad to be leaving, to be starting a new life in a new city, a life of shiny wood floors and white walls and Southern drawls.

Yet I missed you. A week into my new life, you phoned me at work. "I don't know how I got home last night," you said. "I remember drinking lots of Long Island iced teas at a bar. I blacked out. I'm scared. What if I was raped or something?" This time when I suggested you go into rehab, you didn't balk. You packed your bags and checked in the next day. Finally I could relax. I didn't have to worry about you having a head-on collision. And I began attending Al-Anon meetings. I learned about detaching with love, about the need to take care of myself.

A month later, you left as a sober woman. I was proud of you. You gathered the strength to tell your parents to back off about your sexuality. And they backed off. But you still suffered from guilt and depression. We spent hours on the phone talking about your alcohol urges, your depressive thoughts. By the end of the school year, I felt drained. Finally, I found the courage to end our relationship. But I assured you that you could still call anytime, that I was your family and I'd always be there for you.

I flew back to Albany to help you celebrate your one-year AA anniversary. Your friends and family attended. We all listened to your story of overcoming alcohol. We rejoiced afterward at your parents' home. Although they never accepted our relationship, they always treated me with respect and even gave me a Yankee Candle for a housewarming present.

Three months later, the day after Christmas, I called and called your apartment, with no response. Finally, at two in the afternoon, when you could no longer ignore the ringing, you picked up and mumbled that you hadn't slept for the past three days. You told me you took fifty melatonin capsules the night before; you didn't want to wake up. I imagined your body lying flat, your delicate hair matted atop your head.

"Even with the fifty melatonin," you said, "I couldn't get a wink of sleep."

It turns out that two days previously, at your family's home, by the Christmas tree, your favorite uncle handed you anti-gay pamphlets: "When Passions Are Confused," "Rebelling Against God," "The Natural Course of Things." That night, you opened a pamphlet, read a few lines, and cried into a pillow. You decided your sins were too much to handle.

After our phone call, you decided to check into a psychiatric rehab. By the end of your stay, you felt stronger. Within months, you lost all the weight you had gained, got a full-time job working with mentally handicapped adults, felt more in control of your life.

Six months later, we attended the wedding of a mutual friend in Vermont. We drove up the New York State Thruway while singing Ani DiFranco songs and making up chants about your schnauzer, Sherlock. Although our romance was over, our friendship had deepened.

A year later, you met Deb, a Jewish engineer. Four years later, I made a toast to you and Deb at your commitment ceremony. Even your parents wished you a happy life together.

Yes, you still have your moments of feeling like a sinner, but you tell me you're happy. And I'm happy for you. You've come a long way since we met.

I remember one night, a year into our relationship, when big tears rolled from your eyes. I pulled my car over to the side of the road and asked you what was wrong. "Life's too hard," you said. "What's the point if I'm in so much pain all the time?"

I held your shaky shoulders. "Imagine happiness," I said. "Imagine what it looks like, feels like."

"I can't imagine ever being happy," you said. "It's not part of my universe."

There are days when I have a hard time imagining my own happiness, days when I call you to seek out answers, when you listen, give nonjudgmental advice, pray for me when my vision is clouded by muffled shades of gray, grays similar to the eye of the orange cat I dreamt about just after we met, the sickly eye that transformed into a sparkling sphere of color, the eye that has reflected your wisdom, wisdom I hadn't noticed at first, wisdom that helped us unearth a lost language of lox, a language instinctual as salmon swimming upstream, fluid as blood pumping to the heart, and we all know you can't change the direction of blood.

With love and lox,

Lori

plain as the nose on my face

BY SARAH BOWEN SHEA

ear Stacey,

Even though it's been thirty years, I still vividly remember how we spent our eighth grade together. The black Calvin Klein jeans and blue oxford button-down shirt you wore on your first day as the new kid at our junior high. Passing you a Starburst fruit chew as a means of introduction. Making up dance routines to songs from *The Muppet Movie* (our answer to *High School Musical!*). Riding the bus to go shopping at Bloomingdale's. Drinking chocolate Fribbles at Friendly's. Sitting out on your roof.

And you making fun of the bump in my nose. Repeatedly. You'd run your finger down the slope of your perfect little bunny nose and then wonder aloud what caused the bump on the bridge of my nose. The bump I'd noticed, sure, but hadn't paid much attention to. (Heck, I was just so relieved to have jettisoned my bifocal glasses two years before that I fancied I looked kinda hot!)

As if that wasn't enough, your whole family would get in on the act (putting the "fun" back in "dysfunctional," I suppose) when I'd stay over for dinner. First your dad would start in, saying how maybe some people would consider my profile to be Roman, like on some ancient coin. Then your stepmom would chime in, pointing out that, no, most Roman noses were just strong, not beset with a bump. Your brother—who had a button nose like yours—would jump on the bandwagon and throw in a few wisecracks.

Why I sat there and took it is beyond me. Maybe because I'd never been at a family dinner table where insults were thrown like punches.

But the critical remarks weren't confined to your dining room. Oh, no, they needed a much wider audience to hit their mark. I achingly remember you revisiting the subject as we waited after school for our bus. As I'm sure you recall, dear Scott was on our bus. Scott, my first boyfriend, even though we'd hardly ever made out. Scott, the adorable blond-haired, green-eyed boy who brought out such envy in you. You wanted Scott as your own, so what better way to prompt him to break up with me than to call his attention to my imperfect nose? But Scott didn't even seem to hear your "Sarah's so pretty—too bad about her bumpy nose" comments. Maybe it hit too close to the bone for him, since he had a been-broken, Liam Neeson-esque nose himself.

Those public barbs were the ones that wounded my ego the most. Even though I realized on some level what was driving you, the comments still made a lasting mark. I entered high school feeling self-conscious about my nose, the bump looming larger in my mind than on my face. Even in college, when I started dating a movie star–handsome man, I wondered how he could think I was beautiful when I had such a schnoz.

Hell, I'm in my early forties now, and when I meet new people, I sometimes still hear your berating comments reverberating in my head. But now I realize why you had to tear me down: You resented the fact that I was naturally slender while you battled with your weight. You longed to have wavy blonde hair and blue eyes like me instead of pin-straight brown hair and brown eyes. (This was, after all, the era when Farrah Fawcett and Christie Brinkley defined beauty.) You wished your parents were as happily married as mine were (and still are). You were lashing out from a place of weakness, a feeling of jealousy. Making your best friend feel bad about herself made you feel good about yourself. I see now where you were coming from. I just wished you'd stayed there instead of making me feel like crap about the most prominent feature on my face.

Sincerely,

Sarah

twenty years, later

BY JUDY SUTTON TAYLOR

ear Allie,

I'm thinking about you again today.

But of course I'm thinking about you; it's December 21, 2008. It's the twentieth anniversary of the day you died. Twenty years, too, since you were twenty years old.

I'm back at Syracuse University this weekend, with Michele and some other friends, to remember you and to commemorate the day that changed the rest of our lives.

Even after all these years, though, I don't just think of you during ceremonies and anniversaries. I think of you all the time.

We were sophomores at Syracuse when we met through my roommate Michele, whom you'd grown up with in Connecticut. We all drank together at the bars on Marshall Street. We saw U2 play at the Dome. We got high a few times.

he last time I saw you, during our junior year, we all slept
at my parents' place in NYC after we rang in New Year's
1988 with Michele and a bunch of other friends. I was about to
leave for a semester in London, for the same program you were
going to participate in the following September. We talked a little
that night about how psyched we both were, but I didn't think
much about our conversation until later. None of us knew then,
of course, that this particular New Year's would be your last.
That I'd return from London, but you wouldn't. None of us could
have dreamed, in the worst of nightmares, that just shy of a year
later, your plane would be blown out of the sky over Lockerbie,
Scotland. That the explosion, orchestrated by Libyan terrorists,
would kill you and 269 other people—34 other SU students—on
that 747 and on the ground below.

No one on campus was prepared for what was about to hit
us on that crazy-cold, gloomy December day while we studied
for the last of our finals before winter break. The news about
Pan Am 103 flashing across TV screens. The blur of chaos and
confusion as we tried to get answers about who was on the plane
and what exactly had happened. The hasty service at the school
chapel that night, which everyone sat through like zombies.

Before the news, our worries that morning were the kinds
that twenty-year-old college kids are supposed to have: about
how to transform a semester's worth of skipped classes into a
decent grade, about boys, about having enough beer money. We
weren't ready for a brutal, smack-in-the-face introduction to how
cruel and complicated the world could be. We weren't ready to
worry about going to funerals (lots of them), about understanding global terrorism, about surreal things like how dead friends

can suddenly mean college kids have to come up with a few hundred more dollars a month for rent next semester because they're down a housemate.

But all of that changed when I went down to the TV room in our sorority house to take a study break just as Michele ran out screaming, "Oh my god, Allie's supposed to come home today!"

We weren't ready for the photographers who climbed through sorority- and frat-house windows to get pictures of students crying for the morning paper, or for the reporters who scowled at the privileged private-school kids sobbing over their dead friends. I was standing next to Michele when she talked with a reporter. "I just hope she's not in any pain," she said. He just flipped his notebook closed and rolled his eyes, mumbling, "Don't worry, sweetheart, she's not," as he walked away. I wasn't prepared for that single moment to change my longstanding plan to be a world-famous, hard-hitting, pull-no-punches newspaper journalist.

It turns out I wasn't prepared for all kinds of confusion that would stem from the day you died. I didn't know how to help Michele deal with the pain of losing you, and I didn't know how to balance that with my own sense of loss either. It didn't seem right that I felt so hurt and so hopeless when Michele and so many other people at school seemed to have more legitimacy behind their tears.

But even though you and I didn't know each other that well, I couldn't get you out of my head. I couldn't help but wonder how your time abroad compared with my own amazing experience just one semester before you. I couldn't help but think about all the great stories you didn't get to share with Michele, the presents you didn't get to give her. I wondered whether we'd had the same professors or hung out at the same pubs or spent the same sorts of crazy weekends in Amsterdam. I couldn't stop thinking all that there-but-for-the-grace-of-God stuff that narrowly dealt you and I very different cards because the courses we needed to graduate were offered in London during different semesters.

I thought about you a lot, but I kept it to myself. The next year, after we graduated, I sat in the Brooklyn apartment I shared with Michele, listening to her sob through hours of phone calls with your mom. I was sad, but she was devastated, so I kept to myself the thoughts I had about what you might have been doing this first year out of school, whether you might have been living in this apartment instead of me. I didn't tell anyone that I thought about you when one of us starting dating someone new, when we went on our first business trips, or whenever I heard a U2 song. You were missing so much, and the randomness of how that came to be was more than I could stand sometimes. But I didn't talk about it. I didn't want to come off as indulgent, or worse, upset Michele even more.

Let me tell you, Allie, a lot happens between twenty and forty. Of course I thought about you through engagements and weddings and the births of babies. (Guess what? Michele has an amazing seven-year-old daughter named for you.) I thought about you when Michele (who lives in L.A. now, while I'm in Chicago) and I shared phone calls about job promotions and buying houses and doing grownup stuff. I thought about you when we dealt with miscarriages, separations, divorces, and the deaths of other friends too soon. During my darker moments, I thought about how it might just be better to live twenty great years and end it there, instead of dealing with all the drama and ugliness of adulthood.

I've thought of you when new presidents have been elected, when I got my first cell phone and watched TV shows recorded on my DVR. I thought about you a lot on the days that followed 9/11, when terrorists took down the World Trade Center—about the countless new families and friends (and friends of friends) who'd be going through similar experiences. I think about whether we would have been Facebook friends.

Sometimes you're in the back of my mind when we complain about how our bodies aren't what they used to be—how we wish we didn't know about sagging, postbaby boobs or premenopausal hot flashes, and how forty isn't really as old as we used to think it was.

It's a different world than the one you left in 1988, in so many ways.

Today I'm thinking about you for all the usual reasons that come with anniversaries and memorials and returning to the place where our almost-friendship started, but I also wanted to take the time to let you know your memory is with me every day, not just today. I'm hoping you stay with me for twenty more years, at least, nudging me to appreciate the obvious and not-so-obvious things that happen every day. Thanks for that.

Love,

Judy

my year as your bff
BY KARRIE GAVIN

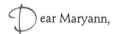ear Maryann,

In sixth grade, the lilac walls of my tiny bedroom were plastered with celebrity posters I tore out of *Teen Beat* magazine. Among my idols during the late '80s were Kirk Cameron, Ralph Macchio, Alyssa Milano—and you. That's right. You.

You see, back in 1987, at the tender age of eleven going on twelve, my proudest accomplishment to date was being chosen as your BFF.

I didn't know what it was that attracted you to me (you could have had anyone), but it is easy to see what I saw in you. I was a mere sixth grader, and you were not just any eighth grader, but the prettiest and most popular girl in school. I was still awkward and pudgy, with those awful triangular, prepubescent boobs, and you were tall and lean, with small but perky, round breasts that had outgrown a training bra. I admired your long, wavy—

or sometimes crimped, as it was the '80s—brown hair and your perfect blond highlights. (Remember my too-short cut that I tried to save with that disastrous perm? I only made it worse when I tried to copy your blond streaks with Sun-In, turning my hair a brassy orange.)

There was little about you I didn't try to emulate, as was embarrassingly obvious by one look at our shoe racks. When you got Sebagos (remember those ugly brown loafers?), I followed suit, and you helped me tie the end of the laces into a perfect twist, as was the style. When you put a dime in your penny loafers, I did the same. When you bought green-and-blue plaid Tretorns, I bought the pink ones, so you wouldn't think I was a "biter" (our word for a copycat), which, of course, I was.

You usually let it slide and embraced your role as my mentor. You taught me how to peg my pants and insisted I shop at Benetton and Banana Republic instead of The Gap. My mom, who shopped at thrift stores long before it became cool, was not thrilled about my new, expensive taste. She wondered why I suddenly became so preppy, but all she had to do was look at you and she knew the answer.

However, it wasn't your looks and style I was most enthralled by; it was your confidence. I don't know if I could put a name to it then, but you had a way about you that made every girl want to be your friend and every boy want to kiss you. I wanted to be you, or at least be near you, so I started lingering around you whenever I got the chance at recess and in the lunchroom. One day, I finally got the nerve to take the empty seat next to you at choir practice, even though I imagined there were lots of others who had their eyes on that seat.

Ever since that first conversation, you started talking to me whenever you saw me at school, and before long, you were inviting me to your house after school and to do things with you on weekends. I was elated, if a bit mystified, but I didn't question why: You seemed to like me and to think I was funny.

I know you liked to get away from your strict mom and spend time at my house with my laidback parents, and I think you liked having someone to talk to about your other friends in the eighth grade—like needy Becca, goody-goody Molly, and fun, wild Nicki, who was the only girl in our school who was having sex (or at least the only one we knew about). We talked endlessly about where she and her boyfriend did it (in the woods?), how they did it (doggy-style?), how often they did it (every time they see each other?), and why they did it (does she actually like it or is she doing it for him?). Nicki probably would have answered our questions, but it was more fun to speculate.

You also talked to me about the boys who liked you, and there were many, but you never had any interest in anyone until Greg came along. When Nicki introduced you to her boyfriend's friend, you couldn't help but fall for him. He was straight out of a teen movie—athletic, preppy, tall, cute, with blond hair and blue eyes, and much more suave than most eighth graders. He was also a bit mysterious, since he and Nicki's boyfriend went to a different school.

When he became your boyfriend, I was insanely jealous. It wasn't that I didn't want you to have a boyfriend; I just didn't want you to have something with Nicki that I couldn't be a part of. You were off to experience this new, exciting world of boys from other schools and people having sex, and I would be left behind. Or so I thought, until you decided to bring me with you.

When you told me you wanted to set me up with Greg's best friend, Randy, I was thrilled. Randy was also athletic, preppy, tall, and cute, with blond hair and blue eyes, although very shy next to Greg. I knew it would happen, because you always got what you wanted. I didn't care that the motive for setting us up was partly to give you an excuse to see Greg while your mom thought you and I were together. All that mattered was that I would have a boyfriend too—my very first boyfriend—and I owed it all to you.

The bliss only lasted a couple of months, but what a couple of months they were! We went ice-skating on Friday nights, and I had someone to skate with during couples' skate. The movie *Satisfaction,* with Justine Bateman, still holds a special place in my heart, because it was the first time a boy put his arm around me in the movies. The other girls in school were so jealous, and for the first time in my life, I felt cool: me, a lowly sixth grader that had somehow found herself a part of this elite group of eighth graders.

I loved having a boyfriend, even if we had nothing to talk about when we called each other on the phone. I dreaded calling him, but I did it so I'd have something to talk about to you the next day ("We talked for a whole hour. . . . My parents were going to kill me!"). But mostly, having a cute guy like me felt like a giant stamp of approval to show the world; it was a dream come true for an insecure twelve-year-old.

But the best times I had weren't with Randy—they were with you. When you and I got home and into our pajamas and raided our parents' refrigerators and rehashed every detail of the night—from what the boys were wearing, to what they said to us, to exactly where they rested their hands when they kissed us goodnight. Remember when we decided we needed to have "our songs" with them? We chose them with no input at all from the boys. Mine with Randy was "I Think We're Alone Now," by Tiffany, and yours with Greg was "Faith," by George Michael. We spent hours discussing our futures . . . best friends married to best friends . . . family vacations together with our kids . . . until, inevitably, it all came to an end.

When you showed up at my bedroom door red-eyed and teary, I knew it was over—not only for you and Greg, but also for me and Randy. You cried on my shoulder and told me he broke up with you for another girl at his school. We listened to George Michael again and again, and you officially changed "your song" to "One More Try," the sad last track where George begs for another chance with his true love. Conveniently, Tiffany also had a sad, longing last track on her album: "Could've Been," about mourning the end of a relationship ("Could've been so beautiful, could've been so right," she crooned.)

The very next day, that would become my new song with Randy.

You told me during recess the following day that you heard Randy was going to break up with me. You wouldn't tell me how you knew, because you were sworn to secrecy. Looking back, I wonder if you just made it up because there was no way I could have a boyfriend if you didn't have one. But it didn't really matter. You orchestrated my relationship with Randy, so it made perfect sense that you would orchestrate our breakup. It was inevitable.

I fought tears at school, and later, with you by my side for support, I called Randy and broke up with him before he could do it first.

"This isn't working out. Our relationship has run its course," I said maturely, as per your instructions, to the boy I still believed I would marry.

At that age, nothing was more important than who dumped whom, a story that would be repeated throughout our school and theirs, and so I saved face and got to be the dumper instead of the dumpee.

That was the one thing I had over you; Greg dumped you, but I technically got to dump Randy, although we both knew it didn't really count, as I sobbed in your arms after hanging up the phone.

I hoped he might try to talk me out of it, but he didn't. We both knew our roles. We were supporting actors in a story in which you and Greg were the stars. Without the two of you, we had little use for each other, or at least he had little use for me. How long was it—a week?—before Randy was going out with the best friend of Greg's new girlfriend?

I slowly and painstakingly got over the heartbreak of Randy. Wouldn't it be great if a wise grownup could have told us, and we would have actually listened, that one day those boys would just be a funny, sweet story—if we even remembered them at all? But alas, we were young and we couldn't imagine all that was to come. (I certainly couldn't have guessed that one day in my twenties I would run into Randy and find out that he is gay. Can you believe that? Do you know that more than a decade later, I still felt vindicated? So it wasn't that he didn't like me personally after all, but just that I wasn't a boy! He was probably in love with Greg that entire time.)

When school let out for summer, I cried because you were leaving for high school, and I couldn't imagine how dull middle school would be without you. I spent a week away on vacation with my family in Cape May, New Jersey, which was totally boring because I was at an age where family is just totally boring no matter how hard they try not to be. But I couldn't wait to get home and catch up with you and have a great summer together.

I called you when I got home, and you mentioned, nonchalantly, that you had kissed Randy while I was gone. You were hanging out with him and Nicki and her boyfriend, and they dared you to French kiss ("for five minutes," you felt the need to add), and so you did.

"My Randy?" I asked, unable to hide my shock.

"You're not mad, are you? I thought you'd think it was funny. It's just ridiculous."

"No, no; of course I'm not mad," I said, forcing a laugh.

"I can't wait for Greg to find out. He's going to flip out."

I didn't understand why I should have thought it was funny, and why you thought it was ridiculous (because you were way too good for Randy, so it was all just a big joke?). But you made it clear that there was no space for me to "flip out," or even to care a little, as if my relationship with Randy hadn't mattered at all. I was so used to deferring to your expertise that I briefly accepted this line of thinking. It was funny that you kissed him, and I had no reason to be upset, I kept telling myself.

But as soon as I hung up the phone, I cried my eyes out. It wasn't just the jealousy of imagining you and him kissing or wondering if the whole time he and I were together he secretly liked you. It was the way you refused to let me have any feelings about it. It made me feel small. Then I started thinking about the way you always called me "little Karrie" and talked about my "little friends" and how you didn't want to see my "little heart" get broken.

You often made me feel small, I suppose to make yourself feel bigger. I realized that was the dynamic of our friendship all along, and I started to see what you saw in me. Surely that wasn't all of it, and some of what we had was real, but that was clearly part of it.

I wish I could say I dumped you as soon as I realized you weren't good for me, but as with most first loves, I held on a while longer. I tagged along to your high school parties and secretly dumped beer in the bathroom because I was too scared to get drunk. I sometimes kissed the boys you didn't want, even though I felt nervous and inadequate around older guys. I tried desperately to keep up with you, even as I questioned the value of our friendship. It was partly because I just couldn't let go, but also partly because I had nothing to fall back on. I had alienated all my friends in my own grade in the whirlwind of the past year. They figured I thought I was too good for them, and I suppose they were right. I was a twelve-year-old social climber.

But it wasn't my newfound wisdom that brought our friendship to an end. It was your new friend Jessica that put the final nail in the coffin. Jessica was pretty and confident and cool, and her hip, single mom took you out to great restaurants and boutiques in the city that you couldn't stop talking about (especially when I was around). She even let you drink wine and have boys over, and you could get away with far more at her house than you ever could at mine. When you started to emulate her style, as I had emulated yours, it was clear you had it bad for her.

The last straw was when the three of us went to see *Beaches* (a.k.a "the ultimate best-friend movie") together. I'll never forget how you sat in between Jess and I, and how you both sobbed (obnoxiously loud, by the way), while holding onto each other at the sad parts. You didn't even look in my direction once. It was a bit like seeing an ex-boyfriend make out with another girl right in front of you while he knows you can see. By the time Barbara Hershey's character died and Bette Midler took in her little girl, I was sobbing almost as loudly as the two of you, as much for myself as for the characters.

By the time my dad picked us up to drive us home after the movie, my time as your BFF had officially come to a close.

*N*ow that I have some perspective on it, I realize that our friendship probably wasn't much different than that of many adolescent girls. At that tender, insecure age, there is almost always a pecking order. Someone is prettier, more popular, and more confident. Someone is the star, and someone is the sidekick. I have been on both sides over the years. I am sure I used you at least as much as you used me, but I have no regrets. In fact, your friendship helped prepare me for the more equal, genuine friendships I am lucky enough to have as an adult, just as what I had with Randy—the first of many dysfunctional relationships with boys—prepared me for the real thing I have with my husband.

You and I were not to remain Best Friends Forever, as we once thought we would, but for one magnificent year of middle school, I proudly carried the title of Maryann's Best Friend, and what a year it was. Today, I have several shoeboxes filled with letters, keepsakes, and photos of people who have come and gone from my life. I can barely put a name to many of the faces, yet I remember you and our time together in vivid detail.

When everyone else appeared to me in black and white, you showed up in full high-definition Technicolor, and when I was with you, I too, was in color. For that, I will always be grateful.

Fondly,

Karrie

dispatches to my salad bar savior: an email friendship

BY JILL ROTHENBERG

June 10, 2008
From: Jill
To: Melissa
Subject: Prince Spotted in Boulder

"Purple rain...purple rain....I only want to see you dancing in the purple rain." Ha. Was last night right out of that movie or what? You in your full-length *Purple Rain* number—purple suede and lavender fringe—so hometown Minneapolis when you actually danced in one of Prince's first videos. Me in my sky-high spikes. Both of us in our getups looking like we made a wrong turn into The Med, where everyone's idea of dressed up is black North Face fleece and Uggs.

I keep thinking that we must have been separated at birth, only to be reunited at the salad bar at the Boulder Whole Foods forty years later. I'll never forget you looking over at me the day we met last April as we both lined our to-go boxes with lettuce.

"Could they maybe put some fresh stuff out? It's not like these salads are cheap." And then the whole line of us, mostly young yoga chicks with flat, bare bellies but me and you in our skirts and boots—working girls in a nonworking town—all in search of the missing balsamic vinegar. What a crisis. Finally, you burst out: "Wait a second, girls, I'm just going to go grab some off the shelf." You were our salad bar savior.

It just gets harder to meet like-minded women as you get older and are single, especially in a place like Boulder where everyone is young, rich, or both. We were that way once here—well, we were young, anyway. Sometimes we thirst for something outside the Boulder bubble (like, um, a bit of diversity, and not just in restaurants). Yet we both love it so much because you can't beat the trails; the running and cycling are fantastic. And as much as we both have a love-hate relationship with this town—we sit in the Boulder Whole Foods bashing Boulder and everyone in it, as we sit transfixed by the setting sun against the Flatirons—we somehow can't imagine being anywhere else. So, OK, I should probably wind this up and get back to work, but I'll meet you at the trailhead at 5:15.

Date: August 17, 2008
From: Jill
To: Melissa
Subject: Snowy Ascent; Stay Tuned!

Hey there. I'm in my room at the Comfort Inn in Colorado Springs, not feeling very comforted by the weather outside. A whole summer of running up the peak at 85 degrees, and now it decides to snow.

It's a balmy 24 outside now, the snow is relentless, and the race is on, at least for now. Pikes Peak Ascent or bust, baby.

Despite this wacky weather, I feel pretty confident, due to all of our crazy training this summer (you the drill sergeant, me the experienced recruit). You helped take me up a few notches, from "Pretty good" to "No messing around."

No doubt it's harder for us now. It's not like we're twenty-one anymore, running up 14ers without huffing and puffing. And I'm definitely not feeling like Forrest Gump on long runs. Now it's all about finding the time as we both balance day jobs with the side jobs that give us joy—your kitchen design business, my teaching and writing.

After sitting on our butts all day every day at work, there has to be balance. You remind me on a regular basis, saying "Okay girl, if I don't run today, I'm going to go totally insane. I'm going to destroy everyone and everything in my path." And when I don't feel like going on a run or meeting you at the gym, I can always count on you to make it sound like something I wouldn't want to miss: "Hey girl, we're going to feel so much better after we run. We can do it social, and Maggie will be there too, so we can catch each other up on all the man drama." Running with you and Maggie—both single moms in their forties with little kids—I can't help but be inspired. With you two ahead of me, I think to myself, *There's not one pound extra between them.* But when I said my ass is the size of both of yours put together, you just responded, "Give me that little J. Lo, baby. I want some of that."

I know you're in Vail for your mountain bike race tomorrow, so I just wanted to say good luck. I should probably wind up this monologue anyway. Let's try to touch base with a phone call tomorrow morning before our races.

P.S.: I just looked out the window. Still snowing. But hey, could this be any worse than the time I ran into a guy running down the trail, holding a large tree branch, which he handed off to me, saying I'd need it in case the mountain lion up ahead decided to jump off the rock he was sunning himself on?! Um, *no*.

August 19, 2008
From: Jill
To: Melissa
Subject: Pikes Peak Ascent: Chaos at 13,000 feet

Hey, lady,
They just called the race because it started lightning. It was actually pretty scary, lots of us running down in a pack. Just heard we made the news. I was at about eleven and a half miles, so close to the top, and was running a half an hour ahead of my best time. On the way down, I had to run around a bunch of guys in a fistfight. One of them was saying he came all the way from Texas to make it to the top. It's like, *Dude, do you want to die or what? The mountain will be here next year.* Of course, a few of us women looked at each other thinking that the boys are nuts.

I feel good, though; it's just a twenty-six-mile training run, right?

Gotta go! Hope your race went well.

August 25, 2008
From: Jill
To: Melissa
Subject: You Rock!!

Sorry I missed your call (I was in yet another meeting, ack).

How cool are you for placing eighth overall and the top woman in your age group? And now you're sponsored? You rock. I know you trained all spring and summer, but you have totally surpassed your goal.

We'll have to celebrate! I know you're going to be doing a lot of training with your team, but I hope we can continue to do some runs and of course hang out at Whole Foods when we can.

Okay, gotta head into *another* meeting now, talk soon!

October 5, 2008
From: Jill
To: Melissa
Subject: What's Up with Us?

Congrats on your new $6,000 baby. Titanium, light as a feather, all-suspension. I bet you're smiling like crazy, and I hope you've made plenty of time to bond with your new bike.

Speaking of which, I got your message, and I just wanted to tell you that I miss you. Seems like we've both been so busy lately. I can't believe I haven't seen you in almost two months. And now that it's getting dark so early, it's a bummer not to meet up every day like we used to.

I know we still have our daily emails. And if we didn't touch base before work over the phone, when we're both about to enter into our little chambers of woe, we wouldn't be able to face it at all. But the fact is, I miss you.

I know we've been trying to get together for a workout or for dinner, but then one of us flakes out. I'm just wondering what that's about. I've been thinking that, as much freedom as we have as single gals (though I know your weekly time with your kids is sacred), it sometimes makes us inflexible. We become slaves to our workouts or to our schedules, which women in marriages or partnerships maybe don't. I hate to say it, but we can be, well, self-centered and narcissistic. This is all fine and good if you're talking about the focused training you need to do a long-distance race, but not so good if you're talking about a friendship.

I want to give more to us, more than daily emails and occasional workouts and runs, especially during the winter. Because you're much more than just a training partner to me; you've become one of my closest friends, even if most of our friendship is over voicemail and email.

Maybe we can try to get together soon, no laptops or phones allowed, just live updates on our latest times, trials, and tribulations!

Miss you, lady,

Jill

was it something i said?

BY CLAIRE MURPHY

ear Helene,

You have moved on. This I know. Still, I can't help but wonder: Did the end of our friendship cause you a single moment's sadness? Did you lose even an hour's sleep? If you knew how many nights I used to lie awake wondering what I did, what I said to cause you to drift away, you'd probably . . . I don't know. Laugh? Roll your eyes? Think I'm crazy?

Because here's where I get confused: There was no betrayal, no fight, no tears. One day our three-year friendship was just over. I *still* wonder, three years later: How could we have been friends-for-life one week and not speaking the next?

In the beginning, you courted me. Yes, I know that sounds weird. But it did feel like love. You were new in town, and I hadn't been here much longer. We were both at home with young children and had husbands who traveled for work. We met at a neighbor's house one evening, and that was it. You started calling daily to "check in," bringing flowers culled from your garden, inviting me to come and hang out so our girls could play and we could drink a glass of wine.

I was the writer; you were the beautiful, talented painter. At first glance, you were the quintessential free spirit who also happened to be the super-relaxed mother of four. You were the full-time mom with the satisfying marriage. You kept a very organized house but weren't wound up about it. It seemed effortless.

We talked a lot about politics. Even though our views couldn't have been more different, we didn't exactly argue. And for a long time—years!—I enjoyed debating our differences. I respected your life's experiences and how they had shaped your ideas, even though they were so different from mine. I grew up in a family where people from opposite sides of the proverbial fence have intelligent conversations about their beliefs, however different they might be. I consider myself a liberal-leaning moderate. I know that you are a committed Republican, compassionate conservatism and all that. (I still haven't heard a satisfactory explanation for what that means, by the way.)

Still, we shared many of the same values when it came to our families, especially our children, prizing honesty, hard work, and manners.

You were—are—always the popular girl. At the top of everyone's guest list. At parties, you're the magnet. People buzz around you, amused by your anecdotes, complimenting your casually chic getup.

Me? I've always been squarely on the middle rung of the social ladder. Well liked, but certainly never the life of the party.

To have you shine your light on me felt glorious. Writing this now, it seems alternately funny and pathetic: Our friendship mirrored the plot for countless teenage movies. Except we were thirty-five.

You were—are—also the mean girl. I couldn't admit it then, but I certainly witnessed it. You were utterly dismissive of people who didn't measure up to your standards of cool and collected. Remember when your next-door neighbor Catherine found out that her husband had had several affairs? One night, after Catherine's husband had left, she walked outside because she knew you'd be out there watching the kids play. She brought a bottle of wine and two glasses, and she wanted to talk. She was, understandably, unmoored.

You told me later that seeing her headed your way, two glasses in hand, was your biggest nightmare. I remember wondering how it could be so hard to offer company and comfort to someone for just an hour or two.

But life in one's thirties gets complicated. Suddenly there are people facing difficult times: marriages on the rocks, children getting into trouble, careers unraveling. And the messiness of the lives of people we both knew provoked nothing but scorn from you.

Here's what I think happened: When my own life started to get messy, and I trusted that I could reveal to you the difficulties I was facing, things shifted.

I was dissatisfied· with my marriage. My husband was floundering at work, not following through with the plans we'd made together. I wanted to work part-time so that I could spend most of my time with our kids, but now we were relying on my income. I was working nearly full-time, raising two children, re-sentful, and alone a lot. To make things even more confusing, I wanted another baby.

Even though I was one of those people with the suddenly chaotic life, I thought that you liked me enough, that the expe-rience might open your eyes. I thought you might, for the first time, recognize that even those of us who seem to have it to-gether don't. At least not always.

Our friendship helped me through my own difficult time, and I am still so grateful for the many hours you spent listening to me sort through my chaos. But I think the life drama (which in hindsight wasn't really that grand: my husband got his career sorted out, I got my third baby, and we are happy) is also what drove you away. I wonder if a little part of you knows that at some point you will be the one who is staring real-life drama in the face—and you're not sure how you will deal with it. So far, your solution has been to turn away from things that make you uncomfortable. So far, you've managed to keep everything on track.

I'm still not sure why I went along with your casual cruelty for so long. Maybe I was lonely and missed having that one good friend, the person I talked to every day, like I'd had in the town I lived in before. But whatever the reason is, I can see now that you didn't bring out the best in me. I had friends who were, in your view, dull. Much to my embarrassment and regret, I ignored some of them for a long stretch because you didn't like them. I hope I defended them, but more likely, I just ignored your jabs.

We still see each other every day, picking up and dropping off children at school and soccer, and at various social events. But the handful of times that our paths have crossed and it's been just the two of us, I literally cringe with discomfort. We make small talk, but it's all business. You don't ask about what's new with my life and work, and I don't ask about yours. The confident, happy person that I usually am dissolves with awkwardness.

Three years later, I like to think I've moved on. But the situation reminds me so much of how I felt the first time a boy broke my heart. I sometimes imagine that he'll—you'll—see me walking down the street, looking gorgeous and happy and think: Why did I ever let her go?

See you around.

Claire

something borrowed, something blue

BY TRACY TEARE

ear Amy,

As I write this, you're flying back to Dallas, and I've just made the two-hour trip back to Portland, Maine. Meeting up in Boston, after not seeing you for ten years, made me feel like I was zooming back in time to high school—minus the stress of exams, boys, and zits.

When I heard that you were attending a Boston conference, I was excited to take advantage of your proximity, and I'm glad I did. Visiting with you, Martha, Marcy, and Nancy felt familiar and comfortable, as if we'd all just left Ms. McLean's algebra class, instead of temporarily stepping out of our roles as wives and moms to resume our teen-age friendships.

It was a rare treat to share the stories, triumphs, and tragedies that have filled in the years since our last reunion ten years ago. After all, phone calls and emails are no substitute for chatting late into the night, over coffee, over brunch, in and out of dressing rooms, and through museums.

But for me, the laughs and heart-to-hearts stirred up guilty pain too. I mean, who else remembers the name of my first dog and understood how much I loved horses? Or the times our Bruce Springsteen–loving social studies teacher got so fed up with our fits of laughter that he kicked us out of American History? Who else sacrificed her beloved burnt-orange VW Rabbit so I could learn to grind—er, drive—a stick shift? Who else included me in her plans every weekend, even though she almost always had a steady boyfriend and I didn't? Who else knew how to camouflage not only zits, but a body wave gone poodle? Who else still calls me Trixie?

All of this makes me feel as low as a street gutter for two big mistakes that I can never undo and will forever regret.

Strike one was missing your wedding, which still digs at me nearly twenty years later. There was a logical explanation. Three weeks before you called, one of my dearest college friends had asked me to be a bridesmaid in her wedding on the very same day. I remember madly checking flights from Boston to Dallas, praying that with the one-hour time difference I could somehow attend both weddings. But it just wouldn't work, and though I had recently made it to Dallas for your sister's wedding, missing yours worried me, like a pebble in my shoe, for months. It still does.

Strike two was far worse. How could I have not included you as a bridesmaid when Matt and I got married in 1993? I can rationalize it by recalling that, at the time, we still wrote and talked by phone periodically but seldom saw each other. After graduating from high school in 1983, we put 1,500 miles between us—you went to Dallas; I went to college in Connecticut and then moved on to Boston. Meanwhile, I had developed strong ties with other great women who were roommates or buddies in college, and I had two sisters who were no-brainers for the bridesmaids' list.

It meant the world that you flew all the way from Texas to Massachusetts to be at my wedding, but I will always regret that you weren't front and center, sporting a blue dress and holding sunflowers next to the others.

I regret it even more deeply now, because midway through life, I know how rare it is to find a reliable, true pal—let alone a best friend. Spending time together recently reaffirmed that for me. It seems like the opportunities to make friends were once as plentiful as fresh air. Without husbands, children, and mortgages, we had time to linger over pancakes or milkshakes, lob lacrosse balls at the park, play the bongos to the Go-Go's in your basement, whisper late into the night, scan the racks at Marshall's— the smaller stuff in life that cements a friendship.

Because you've got a heart of gold, you've never mentioned the sting of my mistakes. I guess feeling guilty all these years has been my price to pay. But it's a small one for a dear friend like you. And if you have felt resentful or hurt, I can only hope those feelings have dissolved over time. Knowing you, you've already looked past it. That's just the kind of person you are.

Always,

Tracy

the last letter

BY KRISTINA WRIGHT

ear Julia,

I don't know when I stopped thinking of you as Jay's grand-mother and started thinking of you as my friend. By the time I married your grandson nineteen years ago, I felt as if I already knew you.

Jay talked about his Granny Wright with so much love and fondness in his voice (how he got his love of reading and history from you; the books you shared with him when he was a little boy; and your house, which he still loves so dearly) that it was impossible not to like you as soon as I met you. I called you "Granny" too for a time, until I realized that word—that very old-sounding word—kind of bugged you. It wasn't how you saw yourself, and it wasn't long before I didn't see you that way either. You went from "Granny Wright" to "Granny Julia" to simply "Julia." My friend.

*I*t was a year ago this week that I lost you. I was standing in the grocery store, though I couldn't tell you what aisle I was in—Canned goods? Snacks? Produce?—when Jay called to tell me the news of your stroke. I remember moving through the store as if in a haze, being in tears on the drive home.

You survived the stroke, but you have been confined to a hospital or nursing-home bed for a year now. Though you're still with us physically, it is your mind—that amazing mind—that is lost to me. I have mourned your loss so many times over the past year. Selfishly, guiltily. You aren't my blood relative; we don't even live in the same state, yet I feel your loss so deeply.

Our friendship began in the early years of my marriage. I wrote letters to Jay's family, both out of loneliness and in an attempt to get to know my new husband—who seemed to always be away on deployment—a little better. His father had died when he was a little boy, and you were the next closest link to that side of the family. You matched me letter for letter, telling me stories of Jay's childhood and of your own life and interests. I began to feel a kinship with you—as if we really were family.

You see, when we started writing letters to each other nearly twenty years ago—letters that increased in frequency over the years to become near-weekly exchanges—I found a part of myself. Those old-fashioned pen-and-paper letters, stamped and sent from your home in Nashville, Tennessee, meant more to me than you could ever know.

The funny thing about our friendship is that it blossomed in a way a face-to-face relationship couldn't. I only saw you a handful of times over the years as we've moved around for Jay's naval career. With you living in Tennessee, and your hearing loss making it hard for you to talk on the phone, I had only your letters to reflect the woman I came to know and love. The woman who remembered events that occurred sixty years in the past with such vivid detail. The woman who didn't travel outside the United States until she was in her fifties, but remembered so much about England that I felt as if I were traveling with you when I finally visited myself. The woman who took care of her family, who wrote poetry, who loved her garden beyond all reason, who married the wrong man against her family's wishes, who raised three sons and lost two of them, who took care of her mother past the age of 100, who loved cats and whimsically added an extra *b* to her beloved Tab's name when Jay and I got married in Tabb, Virginia. The woman who would have liked to be a writer, but life got in the way. The woman who joked that her letters were her "blog," filled with silly thoughts and nonsense.

I treasured every word and sent you blank journals in hopes of inspiring you to write even more. Without prejudice, I learned who you were. I would see current pictures of you, and my heart would reject them. That woman in the photos—with her white hair, kind features, and soft body—was somebody's grandmother, certainly, but she was not the Julia I know.

The Julia I know is full of fire and gumption. The Julia I know is shrewd and clever, always ready with a unique turn of phrase to describe something mundane. The Julia I know makes me smile and think and cry. The Julia I know is poetry on the page, keen observations and thoughtful commentary. The Julia I know reads voraciously—every book I send her is read within days. The Julia I know is homebound, because she doesn't drive, but her mind lets her travel to all corners of the world through books and memories of the places she's been. The Julia I know is not eighty-nine years old—it's not possible! The Julia I know is an incredibly gifted writer who inspires my own writing in an untold number of ways. The Julia I know—the Julia I *knew*.

I didn't write to you after your stroke. Not at first. I didn't know what to say, how to write what I was feeling. You weren't the Julia I knew anymore—you were this old woman in a hospital bed, body and mind broken. Then, a couple of weeks after it happened, I was told you had asked about me and why I hadn't written. I felt awful. I felt as if I had abandoned my friend when she needed me most. How was I to know you would think of me when your mind was lost in the past, in memories that had nothing to do with me?

I started writing then. Not as often as before—it was like sending letters into a dark void, and I found myself running out of words to write without the benefit of your response—but I wrote. Through the family grapevine, I was told you were sometimes lucid and would read my letters then. I don't know if that's true. No matter what I was told about how you might be getting better, how you had good days, how you might be home in time for this or that holiday, I would never believe it myself until I got a letter from you. If and when I saw a letter from you in my mailbox, one of your no-nonsense business envelopes addressed in that graceful handwriting I had come to love, I would know you had come back to me.

That letter never came.

I kept writing, up until a couple of months ago, when the news of your steady decline made me understand that you weren't able to read my letters. It was with guilty relief that I stopped writing you. That sounds awful, I know, but the truth is I had simply run out of words. I had written you thousands of words over the years—my dreams for the future, my days spent in coffee shops trying to be half as good a writer as I think you are (which you never seemed to believe). I told you about my dysfunctional childhood, my mother's death, my attempts to get pregnant, my fear of losing my identity if I became a mother, my life as a navy spouse (and the loneliness that often brings), and how I would like to name a child after you—if I ever have a child. I sent you the books I had used in my graduate classes and joked that you were getting your master's degree along with me. I wrote to you about the college classes I was teaching, and you were delighted to hear about my experiences.

After your stroke, it was hard to write about myself when I knew you were not well or healthy or comfortable or in your own home. It was hard to write anything more than the two sentences I wrote in every single letter after that awful day: I miss you. I miss your words.

I forget, sometimes, what has happened to you. That's the problem with your not being a part of my day-to-day life; it's easy to push it to the back of my mind. To willfully forget the awful reality. To tell myself there will be a letter in the mail today or, if not today, certainly tomorrow. I forget, and then I feel guilty for forgetting. Months ago, the day I admitted to myself there would be no more letters from you, I cried.

I find your old letters in all sorts of odd places. I would often check the mail on the way out, and rather than save your words for when I got home later, I would bring your letters with me to read wherever I might be headed. So I discover your letters tucked into books and folders, jammed into coat pockets and old purses, buried in a stack of bills or holiday catalogs, or even fallen between the seats of my car. Your words are still everywhere—surrounding me, comforting me—and I savor them all over again.

In the first few months after your stroke, the third-hand news we got from the family was encouraging. There was talk that you'd be back in your own home by spring. You love your plants and flowers so much, it seemed fitting that you would blossom into your old self as the flowers were blooming in your yard.

It wasn't to be. The months slipped by, and spring came and went, then summer, and you were still not yourself. You were lost in the past, and I was thankful that your mind—that amazing mind—seemed to be protecting you from your current situation by letting you relive happier days. Autumn came, then your birthday, then the holidays—and the news is still increasingly grim.

You won't be coming back to me. Soon I will be mourning your loss all over again.

It's ironic that the last letter I received from you was at the end of last year. It was after Christmas, just days before your stroke, and you wrote about the holidays, the cold weather, the coming year. Your letter had a pensive tone—perhaps due to the dreary weather or the postholiday solitude—but there was an underlying yearning for spring. You wrote about the future, not knowing that just a few days later, your life would be a jumble of medical tests and antiseptic rooms and unfamiliar surroundings away from your beloved home and books and jungle of plants brought inside for the winter.

In that last letter, which I have read so many times, you wrote to me that you had "much to think on" in the new year.

If only I knew, I would have written you every day instead of a few times a month. I would have sent you more books—so many more books!—instead of rationing them so that you didn't get overwhelmed. (Truth is, I don't think it was possible to overwhelm you with books.) I would have sent you pictures from my trips to London and Bath—I sent you a few, but I meant to send more when you asked for details, always hungry for information about history and about England.

I feel guilty for not doing more, for not writing as often as I thought about you. Because I thought about you—still think about you—every day. I read book reviews or pick up books in the bookstore and think, "Julia will love this!" and then reality strikes. You won't be reading any more books. You won't be writing any more letters.

I won't be writing any more letters either, Julia. This is my last letter to you. How my heart breaks to know you will never read it or understand what it means to me to write it. You helped me find myself in those letters we wrote to each other. Writing to you, slowly and methodically, with my pen scratching on stationery instead of my fingers clicking on a keyboard, gave me time to think about what I really wanted to say. With every letter, I tried to show you who I really was by measuring my thoughts and choosing my words carefully.

You knew me in a way no one does—and I feel as if I knew you in a different way than anyone could. We are friends, you and I, and I am honored to call you so.

I will always miss you, Julia. I will always miss your words. Thanks for letting me know you through your letters—and for helping me find myself through mine.

Much love,

Kris

when words fail

BY CELENA CIPRIASO

ear Lee,

You were tall. That's what I first noticed about you. That and your backwards Red Sox hat. As an Orioles fan myself, I wasn't sure if I could like you, so I kept my distance.

We didn't speak for those three weeks at writer's camp at UVA. Instead, we eyed each other from across the room, we heard each other's name in conversation, and we knew each other by height: You were the tallest; I was the shortest. You were one of the older kids, having just graduated high school, while I was one of the younger kids, just about to start my junior year. You seemed older and quiet, while I was loud and rambunctious.

We didn't speak to each other until the last night, when we were each wandering from floor to floor, passing around our writer's camp "yearbook," collecting the signatures of strangers who briefly became close friends and who would be strangers again by the next day, promising that we would K.I.T. We passed each other in the hall. "I hate the Sox," I admitted to you. You replied, "Well, if all we had were friends that were just like us, life would be boring." I think this made me immediately like you.

You asked me if I wrote letters and I told you, "Not well, but I can always get better." And you told me that you were a great letter writer, maybe one of the best, that you would write me great letters if I wrote you back. I didn't question why we agreed to write letters to people we barely knew back then, but that's what you did when you were sixteen and at writer's camp looking for other writer friends. We exchanged addresses and spent hours talking that night.

Time blurs memory, and I don't remember what words we shared, but I do remember thinking, "I really like this tall kid." And then we left Virginia behind, returning to our normal lives—you to Massachusetts, me to Maryland.

Within the first month, you sent me a letter, a great letter. It was long, your handwriting was cramped, and I learned you loved Led Zeppelin's "Stairway to Heaven." You asked if I'd ever heard of it, so I went on the Internet and looked up the band. I wasn't really sure if they would be something I would like—they sounded like a band only boys would like.

I wrote you back, telling you that I liked Fiona Apple and Fleetwood Mac, but I didn't really know this band named Zeppelin. With the next letter you sent, there was a box; you had made me a mixed tape with "Stairway to Heaven" as its first track. You told me that this was a song to hear alone, and that the first time I heard the song, I wouldn't fully hear it; that I would only feel it, sense its mood. That I should close my door to my room and just hear and feel it. And that once I did that, I would understand that Zeppelin speaks to everyone.

I wasn't sure what that meant, so I did what you told me: shut my door and just let the music play. As the music filled the room, I thought of you, sitting in your room alone, like me, and I wondered if you felt as I did—alone, reaching, those teenage years lasting forever, the loneliness spanning before us, and wondering, just wondering, if there was a person out there who understood this same feeling.

Letters came monthly, sometimes more often, and they were always long, always poetic, always full of your ideas and your thoughts, excerpts of your writing. You spoke of your life in Worcester. You told me that you didn't have many friends, but the friends you had you were loyal to, if they were loyal to you. But somehow, in between your stories—your dreams of going off to college later that summer elsewhere in Massachusetts, of remaining a writer—somehow, each time I finished your letter, I felt you were covering a feeling with your words, something that was lost and incredibly lonely. I had never been to Massachusetts, but with your words, I imagined your cold winters, the bare trees, the bundled clothes against the wind. You told me that while you hated the cold, you loved what winter brought: hot chocolate and marshmallows; reasons to stay in and read long books.

I tried to paint for you my life in Maryland—how I loved the Inner Harbor and the Aquarium, and how I hated the long roads, the distance we had to travel from one place to the next. How I loved Memorial Stadium but wasn't sure if I would love Camden Yards because it felt like Baltimore was trying to replace my youth. We were both baseball fans—I tried not to hold it against you that you loved the Sox, and you promised not to hate me for the Orioles having won a more recent world championship. You told me that I made Maryland seem like a museum, a place people may want to visit but never really live. And I told you, "You have summed up how I have felt for most of my life."

And I wrote to you, "I wish we had lived in the same town growing up. I think we would have been best friends, maybe a little less lonely." You responded, "We meet people when we should. We know each other now. Maybe we'll know each other for a long time."

I tried to keep up with you, to fill my letters with as many funny stories as possible, but your letters always outmatched mine in consistency and frequency. I convinced you that the phone was a necessary evil, just as good as letters, but even better in a way, because we could hear each other's voices. You finally conceded, and we began to speak. I learned your voice was nothing like I imagined it sounding over static lines, but through our phone conversations—as we talked about our struggles to figure out what to do with our lives—our friendship deepened beyond letters.

One night, I felt an overwhelming need to call you, and when you answered, you asked, "How did you know to call?" You told me—simply, sadly—that your grandfather had just died. And later, right after a boy broke my heart, you called me that very night and told me, "I felt this need to call you."

No one had ever known to reach out to me like you did. We lived hundreds of miles apart, we saw each other only a handful of times over the six years we were friends, but we knew we could depend on each other when we didn't even know that we needed someone.

Do you remember how we made a pact to try to see each other once a year? That first visit, you drove down to visit me in Maryland and stayed at our house, and I attempted cooking for the first time by making scrambled eggs for you. While they came out a little runny, I was proud of the first breakfast I'd ever made, and you were proud of me for trying. That second visit, once you were in college, I went up to Massachusetts and stayed in your dorm room. You showed me your college life, and you were quietly proud that you were earning your college degree all on your own, and I was proud of you.

Our lives moved forward, but the letters continued. I moved to New York for college; you were on the verge of finishing school, on your way to moving to another Massachusetts town. But we always remembered each other.

We hated each other's politics. I was a staunch liberal. You were a hesitant conservative. You thought people took the First Amendment too liberally when I thought you couldn't take it liberally enough. You saw a reason for the Iraq War, but I argued that I had witnessed 9/11 myself, saw the towers crashing outside my window, and that nothing I saw had to do with Saddam Hussein. We would debate, but we never let politics stand in the middle of our friendship. I don't think I ever told you that you were the only conservative person I could ever tolerate.

When I was trying to run away from the boy I lost my virginity to, you gave me a place to run to. You took me on my first road trip when we drove across Massachusetts. Remember how we threw our things into a car, found a random hotel room on the road, and stayed up all night drinking beers? And when you heard me weeping in the night, you reached across our beds, held my hand, and stroked my hair until I slept. I could tell you things that I couldn't tell the people I called my best friends. I told you how much blood there was after I first had sex, how much I wanted to believe that I was in love, yet I never felt beautiful when I was with this boy. In fact, it seemed that all he could see was what was *wrong* with me. But at the time, I didn't want to acknowledge that I had lost my virginity to a boy that couldn't care less about me.

You did what no one else would do, what I needed the most—you didn't give me advice, you didn't judge me or call me naive. You simply held my hand.

When your oldest friend disappeared without a word, you called me at all times of the day, wondering where she could be, if she was okay. You told me how you stopped by her place and realized that she had moved. You tried to call her phone, but she had disconnected the line. And you didn't want to face the fact that she had left without a word, without telling you where she was going. You told me how you might never know where she had gone, or why she never even told you why she was leaving.

I just listened to you because I know you missed her, and while I knew that I would never take her place, I tried to remind you that I would never be like her—that I would never leave you. And when I promised you that, I meant it. I couldn't imagine hurting you the way you were hurting in that moment.

I was scared to tell you that I was leaving to study in Italy, but when I finally told you, you were supportive, as always. Even though you hated computers and preferred handwritten letters, you decided to start using email just to get emails from me. You became part of a mass email I sent when I got hit by a car. When I returned, we didn't speak for a few months, and I realized that I had forgotten you, something that I promised I would never do. I called you, and you were distant, cool. When I asked what was wrong, you told me, "When you got hit by the car and sent that email to everyone, I was mad. You could have been hurt. You *were* hurt. I'm not a mass email." And I knew you were right and I was sorry.

Then I told you my news. I had fallen in love with an American boy I met at the study-abroad program in Italy, a boy who went to NYU like I did.

I heard you whoop into the air, and say, "I knew it! I had a feeling! Tell me everything!" You loved love stories. You loved hearing all the details as much as I loved telling them. You never got annoyed about the little things that amazed me about being in love—how amazing it was to curl around someone's body at night, how breathtaking it was to trace over the lines of your loved one's face in the morning. You loved to tell your own love stories. You catalogued details as much as I did. You remembered every moment that made a person beautiful to you. You forgave people's mistakes; you gave people reasons and histories for breaking your heart, even if you barely knew them. And even if a boy broke your heart, you still remembered the reason you loved him in the first place. That was the dreamer in you. And I understood that, because I did the same thing. That was the writer in us.

"I want you to find love," I remember telling you. And you would tell me, "I know it's out there waiting for me." And it always broke my heart a little when you would say those words, because I heard the catch in your voice. I know how much you hoped, and how it could sometimes hurt. But you loved love too much not to be happy for me.

It took years to convince you to visit me in New York. You despised cities, but I wanted you to see my life now, to meet my love. And you knew how important it was to me, so you came. And when you did, everyone got along. We ate an Italian meal, we had wine, we spoke long into the night. And before we all went to bed at my place, you told me, "He's good enough for you."

When you left that last time, I didn't know it would be the last time I saw you. Perhaps you did. I stood by your car as you packed it up, ready to go back to Massachusetts. You reached out to me and took my hands in your hands, kissing my cheek, and told me, "I'm happy for you."

Months passed, and you sent a letter, maybe two. I was working in theater by now, trying to make a living as a writer. I was in love, living a life that made me forget the life we had over letters and emails and phone calls. I don't know when I started forgetting to write you, when the days became months and the months became years.

I just remember that years later, I woke up beside my boyfriend feeling lost. He asked what was wrong, and I couldn't place into words what I felt was missing. It was only later in the day, when I was cleaning my room and came across your last letter to me, that I remembered.

I had dreamed about you, and we were talking, talking like we always did, over the phone, into the night. I dreamed that I wrote you letters and letters, that we were still friends, as close as we had always been, as close as we always thought we'd be. I still have that dream every once in awhile.

I don't know why I never wrote that letter, made that call to you, why I stopped trying. I don't know why I broke my promise to you. It's one of the things I'm trying to make right now, six years later, but it's not as easy as it sounds. I've Googled your name, but I haven't found you. I've left messages at your parents' house, but they've gone unanswered.

Because I don't know where you are and how you're doing, I think of you now, and I imagine that you've found that person to curl your body around at night, that person you love to wake up to in the morning. I imagine that you laugh more times than you frown. I imagine everything being good and honest and true in your life, because that's everything that you are and everything that you deserve.

I don't know what makes us forget the people that were so important to us. Maybe it was distance, but that excuse seems too easy. I think I didn't realize how rare and special it was to have someone like you in my life, someone so similar yet different from me, someone who knew when I needed her without words. I think I just took that for granted, and that if I forgot you for a time, you would always just be there again, waiting, easy to connect with, easy to find.

But life doesn't work that way. People don't wait around for others to realize their mistakes. I know it's selfish of me to hope that when you remember me, you remember the better times, the closer times of our friendship before I hurt you. But I do hope.

So this is all I can do. Write this last letter to you. Write this now and hope it'll reach you. And maybe you'll be in a bookstore and be drawn to this book for some reason, and you'll recognize my name, and you'll see my words to you, and you'll know just how much you meant to me—even if it might be too late. And I'll hope that maybe you'll forgive me and reach out.

This time, I'll write back.

Love,

Celena

the mommy wars
killed our friendship

BY SHANNON HYLAND-TASSAVA

ear J.,

When we first became friends—almost two decades ago, as college-student preschool assistants—we were taking care of other people's children. Who would have thought that, years later, the care of our own children would lead to the downfall of our friendship?

It's easy to be fast friends at twenty. The things young women bond over at that age are achingly low-stakes compared to all that comes later. Parties, part-time jobs, boys: a million little distractions on the way to full-time adulthood. Now, as a thirtysomething married mother of two, a former career woman turned contented stay-at-home mom, I know all that stuff is inconsequential. It's the mommy wars that really test a friendship.

Of all the shocking truisms of parenting that no one tells you about before you have that first baby—and there are so many! — the most surprising for me was the fact that parenthood would cause me to lose friends. Who knew? No one warns you about these things when you're newly pregnant and consumed only with hazy-sweet images of pastel crib bedding and impossibly tiny newborn diapers. No one takes you aside and says,

Listen, there are a few things you should prepare yourself for. Pooping on the delivery table could very possibly occur. After childbirth, you probably will not have sex with your husband again for a very, very long time; far longer than the mythical "six weeks." Breastfeeding is complicated and could require a team of experts to teach you how to do it properly. Some of your current friends will turn on you, and everything you think you know about friendship will go out the window.

But they really should. It would have been nice to have a little advance warning.

There are two ways a friendship can go south once babies enter the picture. First, there's the friend who remains childless while one moves onward into pregnancy, babies, and parenting, and who can no longer relate to the new parent. Where once one was free to meet her for movies and brunch—to converse about more than growth-chart percentiles and vaccinations—now this friend can scarcely comprehend the new language of parenting, and there's little time or energy for a coherent conversation to- gether, let alone a sit-down restaurant meal. The result, some- times, is that this friend gradually fades into the background of one's new-parent life until she's not really there anymore at all and the friendship takes on the aura of something past. It may rekindle if this friend becomes a parent herself down the road, though sometimes even then the timing's just not right.

This particular friendship failure is at least understandable; after all, who can blame a freewheeling non-mama for reacting with bemusement to the whirlwind existence of new parenthood as witnessed from afar? No woman—not even the most well-intentioned one—ever knows what parenting is like until she's in the thick of it. Inexperience limits understanding, and if you don't understand someone, you can't be a very engaged friend, no matter how hard you try to *ooh* and *aah* at every detail.

The second kind of postbaby friendship meltdown is the sneakier, more passive-aggressive variety. That's when a covertly insecure fellow-mom friend either disapproves of one's parenting lifestyle (because it's not an exact replica of, and therefore doesn't validate, her own) and finds subtle ways to say so, or she willfully misinterprets expressions of satisfaction with one's own differing parenting decisions as criticisms of her disparate choices. ("I'm so happy staying home with my children" becomes, to her ears, "You are wrong not to be home with yours.")

Sound familiar?

Ah, so much fodder for flailing self-doubt; Before becoming a mother, I had no idea! The breastfeeding or bottles debate! The cry-it-out zealots vs. the attachment aficionados! The question of whether to stay at home or return to work! TV for toddlers or no TV? Sugar and Goldfish crackers, or organic health-food only? Nanny? Commercial childcare center? Home daycare? The list of potential mothering minefields goes on and on, and somewhere in there is the demise of a friendship or two, including yours and mine.

Moms can be pretty tough on each other, especially moms who are stressed, overtired, or stretched too thin. It's as if we're all jockeying for position on the Best Mom continuum, eyeing the competition to see who's handling the pressures of motherhood with more grace and style. I've become used to the hypercompetitiveness that sometimes shows up within the ranks of certain insecure moms.

Still, I never expected to field mommy-wars direct fire from a longtime friend.

So let's review a few of the zingers you've passed my way over the years, shall we?

- Informing me, shortly after the medically traumatic delivery of my first child, that I am doing things "wrong" by not training my newborn to sleep through the night at six weeks old, as you did with yours (by letting the baby cry unaided for hours on end in the dark until she learns that no one is coming to nurse her)? Not helpful.

- Ignoring the birth of my second child, sending neither a new-baby gift nor even a congratulatory card (despite the fact that when your second child was born, we—of course!—sent a gift, just as we had for the birth of your first child, and included a big-brother present for your firstborn as well)? Coldhearted.

- Criticizing me for struggling to fully groom myself every day when I have two children under the age of three in the house—a toddler at my knees and a baby at my breast? Snidely mentioning how tired you are of mothers who whine about how hard their mothering lives are; so hard that they can't even catch a shower every day, they don't have time to apply a little makeup—when, of course, your children are now old enough to entertain themselves and go to school and give you ten minutes of peace in your bathroom alone every day? Pretty bitchy.

- Advising me, unbidden, that if my husband and I don't find a way to begin instituting a weekly "date night" (as you and your husband do) away from our toddlers—never mind that, living on one modest salary, we literally cannot afford both a regular babysitter and to pay our electric bill—our marriage is guaranteed to fail? Shockingly insensitive.

- Finding every possible opportunity to smugly tell me how you're raising *your* kids with no fast food in a TV-free home, only to later let slip occasional references to the McDonald's drive-through, PBS Kids, *Cars* and Berenstain Bears videos? Kind of pathetic.

- Spreading lies about me—telling mutual friends that I insulted your working-mom life by calling it distasteful and wrong, when what I actually said was that the working-mom life is wrong *for me*? And then refusing to acknowledge my sincere apology for the misunderstanding while continuing to misrepresent my opinions to other people we know? Passive-aggressive to the extreme.

It has occurred to me that all of these things fall under the heading of "Things a Real Friend Would Never Do." Of course, they also fall under the heading of "Things Only Crazy-Insecure Mothers with Unmanageable Lives Who Deep Down Inside Feel Like Shit Might Do in Order to Make Themselves Feel Better About Their Parenting Choices, Their Marriages, Their Work–Family Balance (or Lack Thereof), and Their Overall Accomplishments."

In the end, I'm not sure why it's so intolerable to you that I approach motherhood differently than you do. Maybe it's because if my way of managing the push-and-pull of home and family is okay, it means that your way of mothering isn't the only right way. Which maybe makes you wonder if your way is right at all.

But that's okay, because I'm done trying to figure you out. One thing I do know for sure is that your constant undermining puts you into a different category from now on: former friend.

Yours in fellow motherhood,

Shannon

true blue

BY JEN KARUZA SCHILE

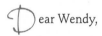ear Wendy,

I still remember the glorious springtime afternoon we met.

"Hi!" you called cheerfully to me from the couch in Chris's dorm room in Buchanan Towers at Western Washington University. "I'm Wendy."

Your face was open, your smile genuine and kind. Your curly auburn hair was pulled back in a clip, and you wore a yellow spaghetti-strap sundress with white saltwater sandals. I remember thinking at the time that you seemed rather like the sun yourself, beaming and bright.

I'd just begun dating Chris, and you had just started dating Paul, his basketball teammate. After a bit of small talk, we zoned in on what was really important to us at the time—turning twenty-one.

"When's your birthday?" I asked when I learned that we were both juniors.

"August," you answered.

"Mine too!" I said.

Turns out, we were born just five days apart, making us both Leos. Then I mentioned I'd just returned from Long Beach, where I'd spent my spring break.

"Long Beach!" you exclaimed. "That's where I'm from!"

Chris and Paul looked at each other, shaking their heads. You and I laughed together in delight and disbelief, talking about the people and things we had in common. Before you and Paul left for your Friday night date, we made plans to spend the next day together.

On Saturday morning we met inside the gym where the guys had basketball practice, then walked out into the sunshine and jumped into my Jetta. We were heading across the border to Canada on a tip about a place that sold fake identification cards. We never did find that place, but we did eat pizza for lunch at a small restaurant just off the sidewalk, and I bought a turquoise necklace from a Native jewelry vendor. We talked and laughed all the way back home, listening to Will Smith's *Summertime* again and again.

In less than twenty-four hours, our friendship was sealed. Chris and Paul who? We were Jen and Wendy: Best Friends.

Most of our adventures took place in the car. We loved driving around together—especially to the Super Store near campus. We'd park on the hill outside, where I'd wait hopefully in the car as you opened the swinging glass door and entered. We always sent you in, because you were the one who had the confidence to pull off an underage purchase of Boone's Farm wine. We remained ever on the lookout for the cars of Paul and Chris around town, sure to catch them up to no good. We dissolved into laughter over all of our antics, reveling in the ridiculous joy of being twenty-year-old college girls.

e spent all spring driving around town and listening to music in between classes and studying in the library. We took my Jetta on our adventures because it was new and had the better sound system for showcasing your amazing music collection. You had it all: dance, country, pop. If it was merry or hip, you had it. In fact, you just sort of "had it" in general. You carried yourself with a winning combination of confidence and kindness, and you possessed the gift of razor-sharp wit.

Paul and Chris may have been big-time college athletes, but you weren't nervous and unsure in their company like I was. (Or if you were, you never let on.) You'd been a varsity athlete yourself, talented in volleyball, basketball, and softball. I admired that about you.

When summer came, we wrote letters to stay in touch until we moved into a brand-new house the next fall with Kristi, Shari, and . . . I can't even remember the name of the fifth gal! We'd return from nights out and sit in your room eating Lucky Charms and sourdough toast in the wee hours of the morning. During the week, we took study breaks to watch *Melrose Place, 90210,* and *Party of Five* in the family room.

By winter, things with Chris weren't going well, but I hung on. Not because I cared much for him, which I didn't. The fact that after nearly ten months together he no longer returned my phone calls in a timely manner was a clear indication the relationship was just about over. What I cared about more was continuing our friendship. If I wasn't with Chris anymore, but you stayed together with Paul, I feared that our friendship and my social life might be over. If we weren't attending basketball games or postgame parties together, would a significant portion of our own connection be lost?

I returned home from classes one dark and rainy afternoon and saw I finally had a message. "Chris called!" read the note, written in light-blue highlighter on a white paper towel. I might have been happy that he'd finally called, but I wasn't.

"Are you breaking up with me?" I asked.

"I guess," he said. "Bye."

I sat alone in my room—cross-legged on the floor, the black receiver in my hand—as tears streamed slowly down my face. The only light in the room came from the pink Victorian lampshade on the antique sewing cabinet I used for a table. I slowly tore the paper-towel message into long strips. I tore those long strips into smaller strips. Then smaller and smaller, until the message was a pile of paper bits on my floor.

Next I silently shuffled over to my closet and took out two CDs that reminded me of Chris (most likely Jodeci or R. Kelly). I calmly bent them in half until they cracked and split. I took the halves and bent and cracked them again, then left them in a pile as the wind blew and the rain poured outside my second-story window.

I found the yellow envelope in which I kept a few basketball pictures and news articles about Chris, along with a handful of letters he'd sent me the summer before. Quietly, I tore these in half until they too were just bits on the floor. Pieces of used tissue lay on the carpet and inside my blue-and-white plastic WWU trash can.

Finally, I lay down in bed. Miserable. Spent. I curled into a depressed ball and went to sleep, waking early to drive to campus. Fortunately, you'd already left the house. I hadn't talked to you the night before, but you must have known what had happened: that I was now an outsider. I trudged underneath dreary skies and through pouring rain from class to class that day, hoping not to run into you or anyone else.

I lumbered back to my car at the end of the day, dreading having to go back to the house and up the stairs to my cramped little room and face the ruins that awaited me. I did not want to look at the used tissues, ripped letters, and broken CDs, only to be reminded of my miserable state.

I was shocked when I opened the door to my room on that hopeless day! I opened the door to a bright room—what seemed a world, really—of cleanliness and order. The scraps of old tissue had been picked up off the floor, and the trashcan had been emptied. The broken music and ripped pictures had been collected, and the floor was freshly vacuumed. A bouquet of colorful flowers sat in a vase upon the antique sewing table, a white card propped next to them. I sat on my pink flowered comforter and looked around, awash in gratitude.

My eyes rested on a shoebox sitting near my bed. I opened it and discovered the remains of the pictures, letters, and CDs, all set gently inside. You didn't throw out my memories; instead, you saved them for me. You thought that I might want to look at them some more, perhaps even tape a few back together, before discarding them altogether myself.

It was the most thoughtful thing anyone had ever done for me. I hadn't cared so much about Chris; what I'd cared about was you and our friendship. I could see in that moment, while looking around the tidy room, that our friendship remained secure.

A couple of weeks later, Valentine's Day rolled around.

You surprised me again by placing festive red and pink confetti, chocolates, and hearts in the dash of my car before I got out to my Jetta that morning. Your gesture took the sting out of the day, and it was brilliant, the way you set it up so that when Chris walked by my car on campus, he'd see the gifts and think I had a new Valentine!

The way you thought of others and always knew just what to do to lighten a heavy heart is something I'll never forget. Although we've hardly talked in the last twelve years, as life has moved us in different directions and to different towns, I still think at times about how your light always beamed so brightly— especially the way it pierced the gloom of that winter day.

Your two girls are lucky to have you for their mother, and I'm always amazed, when I receive your Christmas card each year, just how much they look like you and Paul!

Thank you for being a friend,

Jen

on wings and a prayer

BY JEAN COPELAND

ear Val,

I'm writing you this letter because I feel like our friendship is dying a slow death, and that if I don't do something, it's destined to languish for all eternity in email purgatory.

Don't get me wrong—I love receiving raunchy cartoon emails about growing old and sucky jobs, and the ones with "hey, what's going on" in the subject line. But when was the last time we actually went for buffalo wings and cocktails instead of just typing and replying that we should?

It used to be easy before politics, identity, and values invaded our friendship. In the eighties, we were simpatico—girls who giggled at silly things like our English teacher's sandals or Michael McDonald's "hey" in *Sweet Freedom*; girls who crushed on the same over-the-hill news anchor; girls who sat on the floor of your bedroom, shoulder to shoulder, thumbing through your

Barry Manilow scrapbook. Remember that day we cut school in the spring of junior year and hung out at Fort Hale Park? That creature floating in the tide—which turned out to be a horseshoe crab—fascinated and grossed us out for what seemed like hours.

How did we begin this quiet journey down such divergent paths, despite still living in our hometown?

I suppose the quick answer can be distilled into a single notion: I'm gay and you're not. Not a calamity . . . except that you're Republican and I'm not. You have your traditional family: husband, house, and two kids. I have my traditional gay family: life partner, townhouse, and two cats.

In our hearts, our difference doesn't matter. You don't have any personal conflict with gays and lesbians, as you once quoted from *Seinfeld*: "Not that there's anything *wrong* with it." In fact, you're quite cool about it. You're the one who asked if you could attend my civil-union ceremony and read the lesbian short stories I've had published. But when you tell me—and yourself—you "don't care" that I'm gay, what are you really saying?

Because here's the thing: It's one thing to "accept" a gay friend, but quite another to feel outraged over society's lack of acceptance of our lifestyle. Have you ever considered how every time you cast your vote for another conservative Republican, you're voting against me—against my dignity, my equality, my right to the pursuit of happiness?

Any fool knows it's a toxic combination to mix friendship with personal politics, yet I can't stop one from spilling into the other. After years of struggling, I have finally grown into my identity as a woman and a lesbian. This metamorphosis has made me picky about what I allow people to get away with. I have evolved into a political activist of sorts, dedicated to the movement proclaiming it is not okay to alienate and denigrate gays and lesbians, even though the majority of Americans—egged on by history, tradition, and the last presidential administration— still act as though it is.

I know you've never espoused any antigay bigotry in front of me. It's just that these days, I find it awkward digging into nachos and clinking bottles of Corona with a person whom I identify as my friend but whose political beliefs and affiliation undermine my rights. Knowing you support the driving force behind the ideology that wants me and everyone like me to disappear, slink off, and denounce our very essences, makes it difficult to enjoy light conversation with you without flashing to an image of a star-spangled elephant flipping me off above your head. How could I truly appreciate the hilarity of what your brainless coworker did that day if I've just glanced out the window to see your McCain/ Palin bumper sticker, deriding me from the curb? I know my alternative (insert air quotes) lifestyle isn't an issue with us; your actions back that up. But how can I embrace loyalty in a friend who tolerates such a demoralizing campaign against me?

Am I taking this all too personally? Should I just forget politics and savor our carefree jaunts down memory lane over imported beer and artery-clogging munchies? Perhaps. But I can't help but wonder if you would suspend *your* dignity and humanity for a night out with *me*.

We've created a trove of fond memories together, most of which have retained their poignancy and humor. And as a sentimental sucker of epic proportion, I relish the gushy warmth of nostalgic reminiscence. But while your past may have included some of the best years of your life, keep in mind that a good deal of my past was spent hiding who I was, laughing at reprehensible gay jokes in fear of being discovered, and accepting my place at the end of the line because I was too ashamed to shove my way to the front.

While I have never been a heterosexual woman navigating the choppy waters of home and family, I sympathize with how hard it must be to live up to the role of everyone's everything, to routinely put the desires of others before (and in some cases, in place of) your own. It must be exhausting. I understand how at times you wish you could board a flight to anywhere that's away from the husband and kids relentlessly calling your cell phone, and I can understand how guilty you must feel seeing their faces after you've snapped out of the fantasy.

Do you ever imagine, then, what it was—and often still is—like for me? Hearing politicians and policymakers say with words, votes, and rulings that my love doesn't count, that I should take the crumbs they magnanimously toss my way and be grateful for them? Or worse, when they act as though I don't even exist? Your children attend Catholic school. Imagine the sting of hearing religious leaders say your family's lifestyle is sinful, and that your only hope of redemption is to pray to God for the strength to change who you are. Pray away the gay.

The next time you're standing elbow-deep in soccer moms at your third game of the week, try slipping into my sensible shoes for a moment, just for fun. The revelation might inspire you to at least feign contrition about your bumper stickers in my presence—might motivate you to tell me you disagree with the Republican position on gay rights issues. Tell me the only reason you're a Republican is because they stand for lower taxes, smaller government, a fortified military—anything, just pick any value they espouse that doesn't demean my existence, and I will accept it.

But you haven't done that. And consequently, more and more time elapses between cold ones, fewer and fewer current discussion topics are available to us over appetizers, and all we have left is the memory of what has kept us together throughout the years.

Maybe if we can ever carve out enough time from our hectic schedules to order a second round of drinks and a second plate of wings, we can delve deeper into this topic in person and come out with a deeper understanding of each other. Twenty-six years of friendship is worth it, don't you think?

Your friend,

Jean

what i wish i'd told you the last time i saw you

BY DENISE SCHIPANI

ear Karen,

I'm still upset about the last time I saw you. I know, I know, it was more than a decade ago by now. And it's taken me forever to apologize, but just know that all this time, I've not been pleased with myself because of it. I let you down.

The last day I saw you was a weird one for me. Imagine my day for a second: I closed on my new apartment that morning then fit in a quick visit with you before heading uptown to my office. That night, I was on a plane to London. Talk about packing a lot into one day!

And after that quick visit, I never saw you again. (Except in my dreams, that is.) I haven't even been to your grave yet, and I can no longer keep making the excuse that I'm here in New York (with my husband and two sons, none of whom you ever got a chance to meet, which feels like a big hole in my life—you'd love my husband), and you're buried way up in Maine, near your parents' cabin and that lovely lake. I wonder if it's because going to that part of the world—which is just so beautiful—makes me think of the nagging, not-so-nice reason I didn't see you more, devote more time to you, at the end. When you were dying.

It's because you had other people surrounding you, other friends, and there was always that *thing*, that way I'd start to feel, as though I was a second-tier friend. I know I wasn't *really*. And I know it's a silly excuse; after all, we weren't twelve years old anymore. (Can you believe that we met when we were twelve? I'm almost forty-three now! You would be forty-two, but when I dream about you, you're perpetually thirty.)

I know you loved and valued me as an individual, not as someone who ranked in some imagined pecking order of friends. But sometimes that's how I felt. Like when we were fifteen, and a bunch of you got tickets to the Cars concert and didn't ask me. Or when you all got each other those silly T-shirts with your nicknames on the back for your birthdays, but when my birthday rolled around, I didn't get one.

Sure, I joined the club, but I was a late joiner, and somehow that made a difference. I remember meeting you, early in seventh grade, when I'd transferred over from Catholic school. You had those owlish glasses, and you came right over and introduced yourself in Italian class. Later you introduced me, directly or not, to the rest of the gang. Andrea and Christine, Chari and Maggie and Barbara. Weird to think that becoming your friend at age twelve was *late,* but those other friends—especially the ones who spent a week every summer with you and your family in the Maine cabin—knew you from, what, age eight? Six?

Andrea, incidentally, is the only friend left from those days that I still see. You didn't get to meet her husband, either, or her son. She's just given birth to another. That's four boys between us. You would love them all. Especially, I like to think, my six-year-old, Daniel. It's weird, Karen: He has this sweet, thin mouth tucked between round cheeks. From the side, I swear, there are times when he looks *just* like you. It stops my heart. You too had round cheeks and a small, determined mouth. Why does my son look like you? It freaks me out and comforts me at the same time.

So back to that last time I saw you. It was a cold January morning, and as I said, I'd dashed to St. Vincent's after my closing. I was suddenly cash-poor and property-rich, and I was flying high. I was a homeowner! After the stress and humiliation of the previous year—leaving the home I'd shared with my erstwhile fiancé, the man who dumped me four months before the wedding—I was on my own and living in a place that I'd actually bought.

And what did you have? A warm, loving, utterly devoted husband (which made me jealous—actually jealous—did you ever suspect?), who had married you just weeks after your cancer diagnosis, just days before your first, awful chemo treatment.

When I visited you, you were getting still more chemo, but this was not the same as your eight-months-earlier, gung-ho, all-guns-blazing, first try at kicking cancer's ass. In that eight months, you'd already had several rounds of poisonous chemo, plus radiation, plus surgery, and the cancer's ass was not kicked.

When I saw you that January morning, you had received the news that new tumors were growing—in your lungs, in your pelvis. This was your last-ditch effort.

I remember your face that day, exactly, like I'm looking at a photograph. You always had beautiful eyes—big, deep-brown eyes—and they only looked more intense and fierce in your thinner face, and without your lashes and brows. You said, "You heard?" About the new tumors, about the dismal new diagnosis. "Sucks, right?"

That's actually what you said. I won't forget that soon. Ever, actually.

You didn't die for another six weeks or so, not until February, just after your thirty-first birthday. I could have seen you again. I could have. But I didn't. I told myself, *Next week I'll get on the train to New Jersey. Next week, I'll call her mom or her husband.*

I put it off. I made excuses, but you now know the real reason: I didn't push myself in because I never felt, in all those years, that I *fit* in. The circle was closed. Oh, I don't think you thought so—this was all me. I wish I'd told you that. I wish I'd fessed up for being jealous, for being pissed that when you were in the first flush of your new relationship, you seemed to have less time for me, the sad sack with the broken engagement.

Here's another confession: Remember when we went out to dinner for your thirtieth birthday? After that night, I was determined to just be honest and tell you that I felt ever so slightly abandoned by you in that worst couple of months after my ex dumped me. Never got a chance; it was only a short time later that you were diagnosed with Ewing's sarcoma—a horrific explanation for that weird lump you'd found in your lower back.

Want to hear something sort of funny? When I got back to my office after visiting you, I noticed one of my coworkers had left me a housewarming gift on my desk: a box of condoms. "New apartment, new life!" she wrote on a card.

I know you get the joke, right, the irony? Even though it's kind of dark? I leave you in that dismal chemo room with those awful brown vinyl chairs, getting a painful treatment that has only a slim chance of letting you live, and I'm . . . living. Moving ahead. Flying, literally: My bags were packed for London; my old apartment packed for my move.

In my dreams you've forgiven me for not coming again. You show up at my wedding, wearing the short summer dress and pearls you wore to Chari's wedding, and it doesn't even seem out of place at my autumn reception. I'm always surprised, in the dream, to see you across the dance floor. I work my way through a sea of dancing guests to find you, to grab your hand.

"You're here!" I exclaim. "You came!"

And you say, "Of course I'm here," and keep dancing.

So listen, I'm sorry for my lame-ass junior-high excuse for not coming to see you again. You were always ten times smarter than me, so I bet you know that already. I bet you've already forgiven me. I hope so.

Love,

a crime against friendship

BY SOPHIA DEMBLING

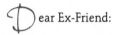ear Ex-Friend:

I can't even remember how long it's been since we've spoken. How old is your firstborn? It's been about that long. It's been even longer since we hung out every weekend, walked together after work, took holidays together with our husbands. They liked each other too. Couples friends are the holy grail of friendship. Hard to find, and precious.

For a few years, we were best buddies. You called me your soul sister.

Then you decided not to be my friend anymore.

"Wow," another friend said. "It's like she saw your soul and didn't like it."

I don't think about you much anymore, but when I do, it's never about the fun we had. It's about how you gut-punched me in slow motion, withdrawing your friendship with no explanation. When I talk about you—I rarely do now, but I did, quite a lot, for a long time—I describe you as the Cheshire cat, fading away until nothing was left but a smile. A polite, inscrutable smile.

I think I know the day that marked the beginning of the end. You were newly pregnant; we took a walk in the park. I guess I said something that pissed you off. This doesn't surprise me. I can be outspoken, insecure, even prickly. I've been known to blurt.

Sometime after that day, I noticed a chill settling over our friendship, and I suspected right away that I'd overstepped somewhere. I brought it up more than once, begged you to tell me what I'd done. I offered blanket apologies. But you turned your polite smile on me and explained that you were just very busy these days. I scrounged around in my brain, trying to think of what I might have said to cause offense.

I seem to remember expressing my fear, that day in the park, that once you had your baby we would drift apart, as had happened to me in other friendships. Babies are evidently a lot more interesting than friends. I was scared.

Was that it?

Or was it the souvenir bracelet I brought you from my trip to New York, the one that said PRINCESS? I thought it was funny, that it was the kind of joke you might make about yourself. Perhaps you took offense?

Or maybe it wasn't just one thing. Maybe it was an accumulation of errors. Maybe I'd been rubbing you raw for a while. If so, you never let on. I had no idea. And when I sort through our past—as I did for a long time after the fact—I still can't figure out what terrible thing I did.

All these years later, though, I no longer care. Because whatever crime against friendship I may have committed, it was petty compared to yours: Our friendship was wounded, and rather than rendering aid, you stepped back and watched it die.

Confrontation is no fun. I know that. You never know how a friend will react when you bring up something that's bugging you. But, as I have told friends at the outset of uncomfortable conversations: "If I didn't love you, I wouldn't bother fighting with you." I'm perfectly capable of walking away from irritating acquaintances without a second thought. But for me, friends are worth fighting for, even if it means fighting with them sometimes.

Nothing and nobody is perfect. We all say and do stupid things. Most of the time, we give our friends a pass. Sometimes, though, we have to call bullshit. If it's a matter of either calling bullshit or ending the friendship, then calling bullshit is a loving act. It says, "I am willing to be uncomfortable, willing to risk looking like a bitch, to save our friendship."

But you weren't willing to do that for me, so I have to assume you didn't deem me worth fighting for. It follows then that all those years you called me your friend, you were lying. And I fell for it. Instead of confronting me and looking like a bitch, you ended up looking like a liar. And a bitch, too, actually. (Guess I'm still angry.)

It took me a long time to get over what you did to me. How could I trust anyone after that, how could I trust my own judgments?

For years, you and I had conversations and confrontations in my head. For a while, I imagined what I would say when you finally called, explained your behavior, asked for my friendship again. Of course I would forgive you.

When I realized that wasn't going to happen, I started imagining all kinds of face-to-face encounters. We would run into each other in the supermarket and I'd snub you. We'd meet at a party, and I'd cut you down with one withering remark. We'd pass each other on a park path, and I'd look the other way. I never did any of these things, of course. I even ran into you in the park once, with a mutual friend, and paused for a polite chat. I didn't enjoy it, but I tried to rise to the occasion.

I guess I can still get angry when I think about you, but I don't think about you often. Too much time has passed. I got over you, found new friends, moved on.

And on the rare occasions I do think of you, I sometimes try to think if there is anything you could possibly say that could entice me to be your friend again.

And there isn't.

Yours truly disgusted,

better than bffs

BY JOSHUNDA SANDERS

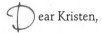ear Kristen,

I'm writing you this letter because I don't think I could ever tell you any of this in person without crying, and we both know we're way too gangster for that.

When I was a scrappy little loner in the Bronx more than a decade ago, I had one best friend. Now, I don't even believe in the concept of "best friend," in part because I know you.

For years, Monique was the one person I thought I could depend on when all else failed. But over the years, I have been graced with the friendship of some of the most intelligent, witty, sarcastic, vivacious, and adventurous women. The list of these women, thankfully, has grown longer.

And your name is at the very top.

Ours is exactly the kind of friendship that I know is rooted in equality and understanding and unwavering reciprocity. This must be what it feels like to have a girl crush, only it is a much deeper, more lasting affection than that. That's why to me, choosing a "best friend" is passé. The phrase itself obscures the kind of intimacy that two friends can create when they don't put each other in "the BFF box."

As an only child with an absent dad and a mom with bipolar disorder, my childhood was complicated to say the least. When I think of my mom now, I think of her walking to St. Patrick's Cathedral in her Payless shoes and her torn stockings, wearing a wool gray skirt and a polyester red blouse that hugs her belly.

She believed the only way to survive in life was to operate from a place of need. She always found food from a pantry or begged for money from priests or foraged through the church's lost-and-found box to find something worth pawning. Any money we got from welfare or from the church usually ran out quickly—a symptom of bipolar disorder is reckless spending, even among the poor—and any of her leftover energy went to finding us a new place to live before we got evicted and ended up in a homeless shelter again.

As a result of this emotional seesaw, I spent a lot of time, hours on end, by myself after school. I knew the way we lived was odd, but I did not find out that it was due, in part, to mental illness until many years later. In the interim, I feared the mean-spirited comments of my classmates, who were wedded to the styles of the times, while I wore men's trousers—and, as my feet got bigger, men's shoes, because we couldn't afford to pay for quality shoes in a size 11.

In public school, I didn't make friends easily. I was stinky, nerdy, and wary of others. When my mom got settlement money from an old lawsuit, she sent me to St. Catherine of Siena school, where I thrived and was intellectually challenged. But I was clearly not seen as part of the middle- to upper-middle-class crowds, made obvious by the ill-fitting uniform I had to borrow.

As preteens, most people are not up to the task of befriending someone with such deep voids I had at age twelve. But then I met Monique—with her milk-chocolate complexion and wide-set brown eyes, standing five-foot-two but with a voice much taller—and she saw something special in me. She saw that I could draw, sing, and write, and more than anyone else, she encouraged me to embrace myself as a young artist, even though she sometimes chided me for calling her too much (sometimes I called two or three times a day) or showing up at her house unannounced.

She may have lived in the projects, but her house was more of a home than mine. I lived, mostly, in a barren apartment about twenty blocks away from hers. We had hand-me-down everything, from plastic chairs with the stuffing bulging out of their seats to a TV set with broken channel buttons. The empty-feeling apartment was starkly different from Monique's, where there was carpet, music, and cable television.

For entertainment, I walked to and from Monique's apartment at least twice a week, on summer mornings and afternoons. She teased me about walking two miles in each direction, but I liked the way it felt to travel all that way without needing to get on the bus. Usually, I would have free breakfast at a nearby public school, then I'd start walking. I liked looking at the outside world, which was so different from the odd stillness in our Daly Avenue apartment. I also couldn't afford bus fare, so it all worked out.

"It's dangerous to walk at night," she would say, pushing a token into my hand. Sometimes I would listen to her and just take the bus, because my feet were tired. Other times, I kept the token, in case I needed it for later, and walked anyway. These were the simple choices of a seventh grader.

While I'll always be grateful to her for befriending me twenty years ago, our dynamic has now shifted. I used to need her and rely on her approval, as if she were a mother figure, even though we were both the same age. Now I have my own voice, and my own home in Texas. The tender intimacy of our sisterhood has been altered by disagreements over life decisions. One time she called me crazy for defending my need to eat five small meals a day in an attempt to lose weight. Another time, I balked at our mutual friend for staying in an abusive relationship, and she chastised me for being too harsh.

When I call her and she doesn't call back for several days, weeks sometimes, I wonder what the time period is for paying back someone who extended mercy to me at a time when I needed it most.

I used to agree with every single thing she ever said; now, when I disagree with her, she sneers at me. During a visit to New York years ago, we took a road trip to her boarding school in Pennsylvania. After several hours of driving there from New York (we argued about her wanting to play gospel music in the car), we sat in a room for hours, listening to a lecture on Quakerism (something I know nothing about). As the discussion wrapped up, I notified Monique I was ready to go and went outside, where she left me standing for fifteen minutes while she said goodbye to her friends. She got in the car in a huff, telling me I was passive-aggressive to just walk out.

"It was time to go," I said, wanting to avoid a confrontation.

"You're so different now," she said.

And as we drove back to New York, we discussed how difficult it is to get used to a friend who once followed you like a shadow and is now following her own shadow. She is content to spend her weekends curled up on a couch watching TV, while nothing would depress me more.

It appears that we have grown apart. And you know all about this kind of situation, you have told me, because it's happened to you.

It occurred to me on New Year's Eve, when I got one of your hysterically funny cards about the case of Paris, Britney, and Lindsay's missing underwear, that we are part of a dying breed. Black women newspaper reporters: There were once so few of us, and as newspapers die, there will be far fewer. But in 2000, you became my only newspaper colleague who was also my confidant and big sister.

At first, I didn't think it was possible, really, to be such great friends with you, since you seemed so polished and I was so rough around the edges. We sat not far from one another in the Houston newsroom, where you kept the neatest, most unwrinkled piece of newsprint, bearing a Mack truck, tacked to one side of your cubicle.

What did we first talk about? Do you remember? Maybe it was shoes. I wear a size 12½ now, and I tell bitterly sarcastic jokes about being a Sasquatch—but you understand, since you shop in that section of the shoe store too.

We were kindred spirits: both in the fellowship program meant to diversify newspapers, both not sure that the experiment we were engaged in would work. We smoked Nat Shermans from the top of the bank building across the street, which made me feel like I wasn't as lowly as the people who smoke Newports and Camels, although eventually I went there.

I have always been insecure, not certain how to be in the world. What I have always adored you for is your unapologetic elegance and tenacity in a male-dominated world. I liked that you didn't seem to give a damn what people thought, because I used to wish I could be more like that: more of an eighteen-wheeler than an old Toyota Corolla.

I admired that you kept your nails filed in perfect half moons, that your Dove chocolate–colored fingers seemed magically shaped to hold pens, so it made sense that you had a taste for expensive ones. You reminded me of girls I'd known in New York as a child: large, confident, with beautiful penmanship. And to this day, when you send me cards or notes, I'm always impressed that your words look like Arabic—neatly pressed into paper, no extra flourishes, not a line out of place or scribbled in a sloppy way.

These are all superficial observations, but they illustrate, to me, the signs that you are a forever friend, someone who doesn't have to rescue me or tell me how to live. You have simply been there, and you have a frame of reference for my struggles: We have similar mama-drama. We both know what it's like to move around a lot. We both are hustlers of thoughts and words and, sometimes, dudes. (On days when I worry that I'm just not polished enough to be your friend, or when I second-guess myself about whether you really want to hear from me about the random vile thought I had about Michael Phelps, you send a text message announcing "I've found the *GQ* magazine with Phelps on it. I'll get it in the mail to you.")

Just when I think that maybe we will have one of those relationships that wanes over time, our weekly morning phone calls lead us back to where we left off. It has been almost nine full years since we first met in Houston—and now you're in Washington, D.C. and I'm in Austin—but still our weekly phone chats continue.

You do not hold my idiosyncrasies against me. You are really like the big sister I always wanted—just a couple of years older in reality, but spiritually, you have lived a wider life than years can tell—and I admire you. That's why whenever I receive something from you, it becomes a keepsake. The note you sent me, with the magazine clipping about memoir-writing exercises? I have it taped above my computer in my office. It is the best gift ever, aside from the wooden model dog you got me, knowing how much I want a real animal and how much I *so* can't take care of a real animal right now.

Sometimes I wonder what will happen between me and Monique. I have called, I have written, and sometimes she just doesn't respond. I have been in this situation before, beating my head against a wall, wanting someone I love to love me back, even when they were hell-bent against it.

You're always there to talk me through it. One night after we both got off work, we talked about how friendships, like all relationships, change. You reminded me that sometimes it's okay just to keep a certain distance from some people.

So here's to you.

In a wilderness of newspapers—where most people who work in the business are older and white—you were my anchor, a template for how to be in a world that looks nothing like us and knows nothing about being a young black woman. When I felt big, big-footed, dumb, sad, or homesick, we rolled up in separate cars at the Whataburger drive-through in our pajamas in the middle of the night to have a snack and talk it out. There isn't a cliché yet to describe this sisterhood, but maybe we'll find a way to describe it one of these Monday mornings.

Thanks for trusting me enough to tell me what you might not share with anyone else, and for always knowing what to say and how to say it.

Here's to a lifetime of text messages, sardonic barbs, and all the gifts that come with a genuine friendship.

Love always,

Joshunda

life lessons

BY V. CALDER

ear Meredith,

This is the letter I would send to you if I could, the torrent of
thoughts that has been building within me since we first met,
ten years ago. Heaven knows I've wanted to say so many things
to you—things that undoubtedly would come rushing out of my
mouth like a river's current, swollen with anger.

The problem is, this is a letter I can never send, for it would
surely hurt you more than it would help me, and that's not my
intention. What's more, it wouldn't make a difference. You are
who you are, and a letter from me or anyone else isn't going to
change that.

Then there's the most difficult hurdle: the fact that you're
my neighbor—a send-over-a-cup-of-sugar type whose kids play
with my kids and whose family shares certain holiday traditions
with mine.

So you see, it's complicated.

So why am I writing this letter today, after so long? I guess I'm writing it for *me*. I'm tired of being angry with you, of bristling every time I'm in your presence. I don't like the way I feel when I'm around you, brimming with bitterness and on alert, ready to pounce just to protect my family from your ill-mannered gossip or hurtful barbs.

Yes, I need to write this letter for *me*, so I can forgive you for past hurts and move forward, so that your negative energy doesn't get in my way in the future.

The thing is, if your words or actions were hurting only me, this would be easy. After all, I'm a big girl. I can take care of myself. But the most disturbing part is that you've also burdened my children with your rude and often confusing behavior—and I'm certain it will happen again.

So where do I go from here? How can I move forward when I know that there will be more blunders on your part? In order to get past this, I think I need to go back to the beginning.

We met the way so many new mothers meet: at our children's daycare. You were definitely nice enough, but your preoccupation with impressing others was evident from the start. You dropped names and zip codes as copiously as an elm drops its leaves in autumn, and you were more than eager to disclose to everyone within earshot the details of your schooling or who your parents palled around with—as if anyone cared.

To me, friendships had always been based upon common interests, honesty, admiration, and—lest we forget—just plain fun. They were not and never would be a way to get into a country club or to be invited to a person's summer house.

But while these qualities were mildly annoying, they were nothing I couldn't get beyond. As you became more comfortable with me, however, I was broadsided with the occasional back-handed compliment or rude statement about another person. Do you remember the time you revealed to me how you and your husband secretly call your best friend's kids "Dumb and Dumber"? Or when you told me that "Jack" had been unfaithful to "Jill" and that they were clearly headed for divorce—a secret that had been shared in confidence? Yes, there were many of those.

As the years went by and our children shared classrooms and after-school activities, I began to be able to overlook your negative qualities in light of the positive traits you had. Every relationship involves some give-and-take, right? It seemed such a dichotomy, though, that you could be both so superficial and yet so frank, so mean-spirited and yet so kind. When I had my second child and was overwhelmed with her constant crying and lack of sleep, for instance, you came over, poured me a glass of wine, and made my family dinner. And I can't count the number of times when, without provocation, you've offered to watch my kids so that I could tackle some errand or simply have some time to myself. I have always known that you would do almost anything to help me if I asked.

I began to have faith that your generous side was truly who you were and that your less-than-noble characteristics were unfortunate byproducts of your upbringing and low self-esteem. In that light, I could surely forgive the occasional foot-in-mouth statement or overlook the fact that you felt compelled to make everything about *you*—like the time you managed to finagle a "Happy Birthday" song for yourself at my low-key birthday celebration, even though your birthday had been celebrated two months before.

It was only after we became neighbors, after five years of knowing each other, that things really changed. Perhaps it's just the nature of proximity that lends itself to conflict. (Think Israel and the Gaza Strip.) But I quickly learned that those minor annoyances of yours were nothing in comparison to the degree of resentment and animosity that could spew forth from your gut.

You'll never know just how much you hurt me that spring day when you criticized one of my children during an argument with me. You shocked me when you said, "Can't Claire get any friends of her own?" and followed it up with "Everybody has been talking about how weird it is that Claire only wants to play with older kids." I felt the floodgates of maternal instinct open, and I defended the actions of my eight-year-old, who had done nothing more than turn down an invitation for a playdate with your *nine*-year-old, since she was already playing with somebody else, someone who happened to also be a friend of your daughter's. Little did I know, however, that my child was obligated to invite yours to play if the playdate involved a mutual friend; little did I know that my child wasn't "allowed" to be friends with any of your kid's friends! Silly me!

I can totally understand that you felt hurt for your child— every mother feels that pain—but the things you said were so absolutely spiteful that they crossed a line. It was apparent that these malicious sentiments were yours and yours alone, and that they had been festering for quite some time. At that moment, you revealed your true self, and I knew that our friendship was irrevocably changed. I learned that day that nothing is off-limits to you.

That was a tough time for me. I started questioning things I had never questioned before, such as my female relationships, and even my abilities as a mother. Why the hell I ever gave you that power is beyond me.

I felt wounded to the core. Although it took time, I managed to get past that incident and have gone on to have some great times with you and your family. Little do you know, though, that what I saw in you that day has remained indelibly in my mind, like a slow and steady foghorn warning of danger.

Since then, I've been guarded with you, not able to truly be myself. I know, for instance, that I can't share anything of a private nature with you anymore, whether good or bad. After all, you continually tell me intimate details about other people, and you occasionally say spiteful things to me about our closest friends, and even their children. If you do this with others, of course you do the same with me. I'm just surprised it took me so long to figure that out.

While there hasn't been another incident as cutting as that playdate argument several years ago, there have been plenty of times when you've bewildered me and my children with your actions. One day during carpool, for instance, you pressed the kids for information about a certain boy who had been kicked off the bus, saying his parents were to blame for his hyperactivity disorder. My younger child came home that day and asked me why a mom would talk about another child that way. Another time, after we had gotten a new cat to replace one that had run away, you asked my children, "Why did you get another cat—so you can kill that one too?" You've also accused my kids—to their faces—of "copying" yours! The list goes on and on. Believe me, you have been the catalyst for many a life-lesson conversation in my home.

It has taken every fiber of my being not to verbally attack you at times. As our friendship has evolved, I've become less and less able to discern which persona is the "real" you. Are you truly capable of being sincere? I've since wondered if those generous offers you make are true acts of kindness or if they're spurred by ulterior motives. In the end, I think that they're both—that you're not capable of separating kindness from the expectation of reward or reciprocity.

Now that I've figured that out, I'm done trying to figure you out.

So how do I get to the next step? How do I continue being friendly without allowing your actions and words to trouble me or my family?

I've finally found the answer to that, and it's been within me all along: As a mother, I need to do what's best for my family, and that means standing up for my children and teaching them how to stand up for themselves—even against you, an adult. That is perhaps the best lesson that has come out of all of this: being able to teach my children that people, no matter how old or young, need to treat others with respect.

So I have you to thank. After all, your unkind actions have allowed me opportunities to teach my kids how to navigate the tumultuous waters of human nature. I now ask them to remember how they felt when you said or did something hurtful, and then to put those emotions into effect the next time they feel like saying something mean to someone.

My kids are old enough now, too, for me to discuss with them the complexities of friendships. "Why are you friends with her, Mom?" they once asked. That's a fair question, considering that I've always told them to simply avoid kids who weren't nice to them. My reply was that, at certain times in our lives, we may be obligated to be around a person we don't necessarily like; this came with the caveat, though, that just because we might not admire or particularly like him or her doesn't give us license to treat that person badly either. I also try to point out the nice things you do and show them that sometimes you have to take the good along with some bad.

So here's to moving forward and not looking back. Here's to starting over and taking each day as it comes. As with any relationship, there are bound to be trials along the way, but from this point on, I am going to try my hardest not to *expect* those trials. I'm going to try my hardest not to be waiting with bated breath for you to make a mistake. No, from now on, with my self-respect intact, I am going to give you the benefit of the doubt. And boy, does that feel good!

Your friendly neighbor,

watching you waste away

BY SUSAN JOHNSTON

ear L.,

It no longer bothers me that you ate all of my Häagen-Dazs dulce de leche nonfat frozen yogurt and then lied about it. Or that you'd look repulsed whenever I ate an entire Lean Cuisine entrée instead of putting half of it back in the freezer behind the frozen peas. Or that you'd mysteriously develop a headache and hide in your room whenever we hosted a dinner party.

All of that makes sense now.

What bothers me was that even after I hid the bathroom scale and stopped bringing home frozen yogurt or other forms of "poison," even after I moved my collection of women's magazines into my room, even after I assured you I would do whatever it took to help you get better, you didn't stop sneaking into the bathroom in the middle of the night to throw up, or eating a few raw tomatoes and convincing yourself it was lunch. If anything, you did it *more* often.

It still bothers me that after several hours of therapy each evening, you'd come home to a roommate who had given up chocolate for you(!), and you'd scowl at her before locking the door to your bedroom.

I wanted so badly for you to see the girl that I saw: the smart, caring, beautiful person who was slowly killing herself and her chances of having a healthy baby.

From the first time we grabbed lunch, during senior year of college, I remember hearing about the gorgeous boyfriend you met abroad and the adorable babies you would have someday. While most college girls gossiped about frat boys, you talked about babies. I thought it was a sign of maturity, that you'd be the kind of roommate who wanted to host dinner parties instead of drunken boozefests. I'd had enough with the boozefests during my year with two cats and three roommates! But seeing you so miserable was much worse than living with party animals. Even after your boyfriend proposed (finally), your self-destructiveness and self-loathing continued.

It killed me to feel powerless, so I brainstormed ways for us to connect without food. I talked to people who counsel other women with eating disorders. I read about ways to support a friend during emotional turmoil.

I tried leaving you alone. Then I felt like a horrible friend and tried coaxing you out of your bedroom and into the world. But the harder I tried, the more you withdrew into your two personal obsessions: food and your fiancé. Both were emotionally explosive topics, but I tried my best to be empathetic. I reassured you when you worried that your fiancé wouldn't actually go through with it, that he didn't want to move to the United States for you.

I even invited you along to potluck dinners and cocktail parties so you wouldn't miss him as much.

Several months later, I was not surprised when you announced that you'd decided to move home with your parents until the wedding. To be honest, I was a little relieved to know that you'd be among family, because I figured they might be able to provide whatever I was lacking.

At the end of our lease, when you came to pick up the rest of your belongings, you barely spoke to me, except to announce that you'd chosen a wedding dress. You described it in agonizing detail, from the dropped waist and ivory bow to the delicate lace sleeves.

But I was not invited to the wedding, and I never heard from you after that. I guess it was too painful to be reminded of the year we lived together.

Even so, I hope that for one day you were able to look in the mirror at your ninety-pound frame and not feel fat. I hope that you saw a beautiful, glowing bride who was marrying out of love, not the fear that she'd never find it. Most of all, I hope that when your new husband fed you a sliver of sweet, sugary wedding cake, you were finally able to enjoy it.

Your friend and former roommate,

Susan

in recipes and cds

BY ROBIN SILBERGLEID

ear J.,

The other night, I cooked those chickpeas you used to make—you know, those spicy ones with turmeric and lemon juice? I loved the way your apartment smelled, the sizzle of onions and garlic in oil. I keep the recipe in the front pocket of my black binder, along with the recipe for Thai curry that I also got from you.

It's been six years, and I'm not quite sure what happened, or when we stopped being best friends and started being acquaintances at best.

Maybe it was the day you packed up your little Nissan for the move from Indiana to Missouri, leaving me standing in the parking lot holding one of your "chicks with guitars" CDs. Maybe it was the day you got married. Or the day you told me you were pregnant, in a too-breezy email, when you were already about

thirteen weeks along. Maybe it was the day I told you I was trying to get pregnant on my own. Or that weekend I visited you,
when your husband showed off the hospital video. The whole
house smelled of your milk. You spilled a bottle, remember? Your
breastmilk stained my shirt, and I went up to the bathroom to
change. Something electric sizzled and sparked between us. Your
cheeks flushed. Your husband looked at me looking at you. Were
we ever alone again?

I never told you I'm sorry that I missed your wedding. I'd
flown halfway across the country to be there and showed up
just after the minister pronounced you husband and wife. I never
told you how I cried myself into a migraine and then cried myself
to sleep before the long trip back to Indiana. I hadn't planned on
missing your wedding—I made a wrong turn, it could happen to
anyone, even wrong turns that take the time of an entire religious
ceremony to fix—but I'm sure Freud would have a field day with
that one.

The truth is, I didn't want to be there. The truth is, I thought
you were making a huge mistake. You were a beautiful bride, but
the woman I loved preferred her college sweatpants to satin and
lace. I barely recognized you.

For those four years, it was like we were married. Trips to the
gym at 7:00 AM before your morning class. Piling into your car to
go to the grocery store, with Dar Williams or the Indigo Girls soft
on the stereo. Nights of Chinese dumplings, pizza with spinach
and feta. We drank hot cocoa and caffe lattes at coffee shops and
distracted each other just enough while grading student papers.
We watched reruns of *The X-Files* on tinny videotapes, curled next

to each other on the twin bed you used for a couch. You cooked dinner; I paid my bills. I borrowed your vacuum; you still have my brownie pan. The truth is, you were the closest thing I've ever had to a partner, even if we never so much as held hands.

(I thought about you when I went to see *I Want to Believe* last summer. Did you see it too? What did you think of Scully's long hair, of Mulder with that god-awful beard?)

*L*ast year, when I was cleaning out the drawers of my night-stand, I found a pile of cards you'd given me. Saccharine birthday cards and postcards from England, where you'd spent your honeymoon thinking, at least partly, about me. After I read them, I put them back in the drawer.

You're always with me. In the recipes I cook, in the black pens I buy at Staples, in the books lined on my shelves. But I feel your absence most at those turning points when I really need a confidant. You weren't there when I miscarried. You weren't there when I gave myself shot after shot after shot and finally found the two blue lines on the test stick. ("All the fertility nonsense," you called it the last time we spoke on the phone, dismissing two years of my life in the turn of a phrase.) You weren't there when I brought the baby home from the hospital, and you weren't there when I named her Hannah. You never even bothered to send a card. You, a woman who had regular coffee dates with a man you called your "benign stalker." You really must hate me.

*E*very year on Yom Kippur I write you a letter of apology, a letter I never send. I tell you I'm sorry I missed your wed-ding. I'm sorry I cried at the reception. I'm sorry I never said

I'm sorry sooner. Most of all, I'm sorry I don't know how to be friends with a married woman.

I wonder about you a lot—whether you've had another kid or gotten a divorce or moved to another state. I wonder if your son looks more like you than he did the last time I saw him, when he was eight months old. I wonder whether you like your job, whether you're happy, whether you're full of regret. In the only pictures I have of you, you're holding your son in your arms, tired and pretending to smile. Were you happy then? Sometimes I wonder if I'll ever run into you at a conference, or at one of those alumni cocktail parties, and find you bouncing a new baby in your arms. You'd be thinner, with short hair, your face gaunt and sunken, all that you didn't choose—a tenure-track job, a life as a single girl, a life with me—haunting your face. I wonder what I'd say to you.

I wonder mostly if you wonder about me.

I have a new job, if you care to know, one of those jobs we coveted in graduate school, an office lined with bookcases and a nameplate on my door. I'm looking for a publisher for my book. I have a house I think you'd love—an English cottage in a historic district close to work. I bought some fancy furniture from Ethan Allen for my home office (do you still use an old door for a desk?). My daughter is nearly five. And I'm trying to have another kid.

I wish sometimes I could call you up on the phone, but I'm afraid your husband would answer. Besides, I don't really know you anymore. You stopped being my friend when you started being a wife.

I told myself I hurt you so badly you never wanted to talk to me again (even if I'm not quite sure what I did wrong). I told myself you were desperately jealous that I got the kid and the job without all the nonsense of heterosexual romance. I told myself I was full of shit. I told myself you were busy. I told myself you just didn't care.

I'm sure the truth is more complicated than all that, but I'll never know. You never bothered to write me back.

Still, on nights like tonight, after my girl is tucked into her bed, when I sit down in front of the TV with a cup of coffee and a bar of chocolate, I miss you.

Yours, always,

what would diane do?

BY MEGAN McMORRIS

ear Di,

I think it's only appropriate that the first time we met, we talked for so long that I missed my bus stop.

It was probably you who struck up the conversation—I was pretty shy back then, and, well, you weren't. I'd always been curious about you, though—the cute girl with two long blonde braids who climbed aboard the bus en route to afternoon kindergarten class, while I was heading home on the same bus from morning kindergarten.

I don't remember what we chatted about, but it must have been pretty interesting, because before I knew it, Fred the bus driver had dropped my friend Cassie off at our stop, and yellow bus No. 7 was already heading back toward Kenwood Elementary.

For a shy five-year-old who didn't like to draw attention to herself, this was most definitely what you'd call "a situation." I had to go up to Fred and, in tears, tug at his arm until he noticed me. Well, I certainly learned my lesson about talking to such a blabbermouth!

The next year, we were in the same first-grade class. And that was when I befriended the girl behind the mouth, and when we established our lunchtime rituals, which would last throughout our entire school career.

What was it about lunch with us? For whatever reason, the midday meal was our time to shine. In first grade, we would finish lunch early, gulp our white milk, and snap our lunchboxes closed, rushing back through the empty hallways to hide in our classroom, stifling laughter as we waited for the first person to scare (I don't even remember if we properly scared anyone; it was more for our amusement than theirs).

In ninth grade—rulers of our junior high that we thought we were—we cut out of lunch early to roam the halls and . . . what did we do? I don't even remember, but every day at precisely noon, we would look at each other mysteriously and I'd say, "Shall we?" upon which you'd reply "We shall!" and we'd throw our brown-bag lunch remnants away and head to the drinking fountain.

Senior year of high school, we became mesmerized whenever mint frozen yogurt appeared on the school menu, and—rather than order a "small" or "large," we amused ourselves by ordering a "little" or "big" mint, much to the confusion of the poor cafeteria workers, who gave us murderous looks as we repeated, "Yes, that's right, a *big* mint, please!"

It was almost like we had our own language—which, come to think of it, we did for a while. In the height of our passing-notes phase in junior high, we constructed elaborate characters for each letter of the alphabet, so that when we passed our notes "in code," no one could decipher the juicy contents. (But since the code was so hard to write in, said contents weren't much juicier than "Hi Diane, how was your day? Mine was good.")

I fully realize that while I'm highly amused while writing this, and while I can hear your dramatic and contagious laugh in my head, others reading this might be as stone-faced as our tenth-grade drama class was during our impromptu skit. Our assignment that day was to pair up into teams of two and perform a five-minute skit using a grab bag of props. Our idea was to perform a comedy based on "Backwards Day." All I remember about our, uh, "plot" was that while I used a banana as a telephone, yelling "Goodbye? Goodbye?" into it, you pretended to drive a car backwards around the stage.

The rest is a little hazy, but I do recall the ending, where we were literally rolling on the floor laughing as the class sat there looking blankly at us. When we had taken our bow, our teacher, Mrs. Landrus, gave a dramatic pause before commenting. "Uh, girls, when you're doing a comedy, the point is to have the *audience* laugh, not to crack *yourselves* up."

We didn't care, though. As long as we were amused, it was even funnier when no one else was in on the joke.

And then there was chorus. I don't know how—or, perhaps more accurately, *if*—we made it through one concert without laughing. I still can't hear the "Hallelujah Chorus" without at least cracking a smile. Somehow we concocted a scenario of how, during our concert, when we sang the dramatic last stanza of the "Hallelujah Chorus," an albino man would run down the stage scaffolding and dramatically swing into us on a rope. (After all, this was in the '80s, during the *Desperately Seeking Susan* era, when an albino man was the scariest thing we could imagine.)

*N*ot only will someone reading this probably not get our humor, but they might also get the idea that we were best buddies. But I think you'd agree that we weren't exactly BFFs. Sure, we were always a part of a larger group of best friends. And you were always on my shortlist for any birthday party or sleepover. But when I think of best friends from growing up, I think of Andy or Elizabeth, while you (correct me if I'm wrong) would probably think of Elizabeth or Lisa.

So why am I writing this to you? While it's not to take away from any other friendship that has managed to take the leap from high school and continue on through adulthood (like Heather, whom we befriended in high school, and of course Andy), there's just something unusual about our friendship that has taken a turn for the parallel.

Let me explain.

Our parallel adult lives began when we both chose colleges in the neighboring state of Indiana (although I liked to tease you that I went to the "only" Indiana university of Big Ten IU, you'd counter that Ball State in Muncie boasted David Letterman among its alumni, which would shut me up).

When we graduated college in 1992, that was the last time we'd live in the same state. I moved to New York City until 2000, and then to Portland, Oregon, while you went to grad school at Ball State, then to North Carolina, and then back to Ohio to marry your husband, Kevin, who you "re-met" years after being buddies in high school. (I love to tell that story, as it's so picture-perfect and appropriate for your amazing relationship with him.)

We'd see each other at holidays or for visits (remember when you and Heather visited me in NYC and we did all those hysterical touristy things? I still want to go on another double-decker bus ride!), and we'd talk on the phone for our birthdays. But still, you were "one of the gang" to me. Not my *best* friend, but *one* of them. You know what I mean, right? I think the feeling was mutual.

And then something happened. Nothing dramatic, nothing traumatic. But when you started working at my mom's and step-dad Dean's software company in our hometown, where you'd stay for three years, I saw you in a different light.

It's not a big mystery to see how this might happen. When one of your best buddies is working in the next cubicle over from your mom, it can't help but change the dynamic a little. The best way to describe it, I think, is that it was like getting Facebook status updates about you before Facebook even existed. Suddenly, I was in touch with your goings-on without getting the news directly from you. And, just like Facebook, it gave me glimpses into your personality that I wouldn't have had if you'd been right in front of me.

Now during phone calls with my mom, I was hearing news about you too. She'd laugh about how you'd proudly declare that microwaved popcorn is your idea of a home-cooked meal, and marvel about how great you were with customer support and fig-uring out problems on the spot. You became indispensable to their company—and it was almost like you were part of the family.

When Dean was diagnosed with cancer in 2004 (he has thankfully recovered), your husband—an ER doctor—made a point to do his own research and visit them with his professional opinion on the different treatment options, as if they were his, or your, own parents. It gave them, and me, some reassurance, some feeling of "we're in this together," that made the difference in an otherwise scary time.

Of course, you wouldn't stay at my mom's company forever. As you got more and more roles in local operas (luckily, I didn't hold you back too much with our high school chorus antics!), you decided to devote your energies to singing full-time. And that's when our lives took another turn for the parallel—and when our phone conversations started getting much longer. Now, in addition to the standard catch-up and banter—*and* updates on my mom and Dean—we had another thing in common: our careers.

While you're a singer and I'm a writer, there are certain similarities in what we do and in how people perceive what we do. We talk about our frustrations when others think our careers are so simple (since, after all, doesn't everyone think they can be a writer or a singer?). We talk about how it's hard to constantly feel like you're auditioning—for that next role, for that next article or book—and how we sometimes feel like we're getting nowhere. We talk about trying to get an agent and wondering if it will ever happen. And because we both look up to each other in a way, it's this unique case of zero competition between female friends, which is refreshingly rare. (Come to think of it, that's always been the case with us. Remember the sit-up competition in our sixth-grade Olympics, when you volunteered to hold my feet for me, even though you were on the Orange team and I was on Red? Miraculously, I won, and it made the victory that much sweeter to know my "opponent" had cheered me on every sit-up of the way! Of course, you also made a point to remind me that the blue ribbon I won for first place should also perhaps have your name on it, ha ha!)

As I write this, the last time I saw you was a few months ago, when my boyfriend and I visited you and Kevin while in Ohio for the holidays. That evening, we drank wine and chatted long into the night. We watched the episode of *Jeopardy* that Kevin appeared on, and you kept pausing the tape to fill in every side story and discuss every question. You both proudly wore your fuzzy animal slippers and laughed at how many pairs you have.

It was the first time Eric met you, but I knew he'd love you guys right away. I was right. When he later described you two to his friend, he said, "The thing about those guys is that they're their own people."

I couldn't have said it better myself. Whereas many people waste so much energy wishing they were more of this or less of that, your "take me as I am" attitude is refreshing. And it's one that I try to emulate, often finding myself thinking "What Would Diane Do?" when I'm having a Bad Self-Assurance Day.

It's hard to explain our relationship to other people, because the thing is, in some ways, we're very different. I always think I'd probably have a hard time picking out a piece of jewelry for you, because you're more of a gold person, whereas I'm a silver person. You're a blonde; I'm a brunette. And we haven't even lived in the same state for seventeen years.

Yet somehow, I feel like every conversation is more in-depth than the last (not that they all have to be; I still enjoy discussing at length who will fill out the rest of our air band—you'd kill on the air drums, while I'm a wizard with air violin!). It's why any emails to each other involve many diatribes and asides, and before too long, our "just a quick note" is three pages long. It's why when you and I have a phone call scheduled (yes, we have to schedule them!), Kevin and Eric know that means we'll be about two hours. It's how I don't worry if I've gotten busy and haven't been in touch for a while, because I know you'll understand. There's no apologies needed with you—about who I am, about what I'm doing. You just take me as I am.

It's easy to think you were just born with confidence and that you never get stage fright—after all, your career depends on your lack of it—but that trip to Cedar Point amusement park a few years ago showed me another glimpse into your personality. I was doing my best to keep up with you, Heather, and Kevin by riding all the roller coasters, but there was one ride that made me draw the line. "Okay, kids, listen up. This? Is ridiculous," I said as I pointed at the ride in question. After you guys gave me your coats, I watched as you strapped yourself in and prepared to shoot up into the air hundreds of feet only to plummet back down to earth (again, might I repeat, there's no need for that experience!).

Heather, being the roller-coaster fiend she is, was beaming. Kevin gave me a thumbs-up, all grins. And you gave me a look like "What am I doing?" I watched you zoom up to the top and was filled with such admiration as I saw your little feet dangling from way above.

When you came back down in one piece, I marveled at your lack of fear. And that's when you surprised me. "Oh, don't get me wrong, I'm terrified on almost all of these rides. I just do it anyway!"

I realized that must be what your life is like a lot, being scared about something but doing it anyway—auditioning in NYC, learning to swordfight for a performance, singing leads that include high Cs, learning a new language for a role, and sometimes, just remembering all your lines. That must be why it's easy to just be yourself with the little things, to show people who you really are—fuzzy animal slippers, microwaved popcorn, TV trays and all—without caring what others think.

So here's to you, Di, for showing me what a true friendship can be—free of competition or cattiness—and for leading by example. For showing me that when you're nervous inside, sometimes the best thing to do is to pass someone your coat and laugh along for the entire ride. And for showing me that if you see an interesting stranger on the bus, it's okay to talk to them for so long that you miss your bus stop. And that it's worth it.

Your McBuddy,

Meg

about the editor

© Josh Alsberg

$\mathcal{M}$egan McMorris is the editor of two other Seal Press anthologies: *Woman's Best Friend: Women Writers on the Dogs in Their Lives* (2006) and *Cat Women: Female Writers on Their Feline Friends* (2007).

Nothing against her furred friends (after all, her yellow lab, Luey, and brown tabby, Lily, kept her company as she worked on this book) but *P.S.* was her favorite book to work on so far, because it reminded her of all of her fabulous (and okay, some not-so-fabulous and now former) friends.

Based in Portland, Oregon, she's written for *Woman's Day, Every Day With Rachael Ray, Real Simple, Self,* and *Parents,* among many other magazines. Her column, Misadventures, appears in the Outdoors section of *The Oregonian.* But don't let that "Outdoors section" nonsense fool you—she's quite adept at getting into misadventures wherever she goes (even when sitting still and minding her own business), which she blogs about at www.misadventuresofmegan.blogspot.com. Her website is www.meganmcmorris.com.

about the contributors

$\mathcal{D}$IANA ABU-JABER'S latest novel, *Origin*, was named one of the best books of the year by the *Los Angeles Times*, the *Chicago Tribune*, and *The Washington Post*, and it won the 2008 Florida Book Award bronze medal. Her memoir, *The Language of Baklava*, won the Northwest Booksellers Award. Her novel *Crescent* won the PEN Center Award for Literary Fiction and the American Book Award. It was also named a Notable Book of the Year by *The Christian Science Monitor*. Her first novel, *Arabian Jazz*, won the Oregon Book Award. She teaches at Portland State University and divides her time between Portland and Miami. Her website is www.dianaabujaber.com.

KATIE ARNOLD is a freelance writer based in Santa Fe, New Mexico. Her stories have appeared in *Outside, Travel + Leisure, ESPN The Magazine, The New York Times*, and *Sunset*, among other magazines. She has profiled Native-American actor and activist Russell Means, BASE jumper Dean Potter, Ambassador Joseph Wilson, and fashion icon Tom Ford. Her feature about world-champion freestyle kayaker and entrepreneur Eric Jackson, "Alpha Geek," received honorable mention in *Best American Sports Writing 2008*. Her travels have taken her to Australia, Iceland, the South Pacific, Europe, and throughout North America. In the field, she's partial to total-immersion reporting: While on assignment, she once ran a marathon; another time, she accidentally climbed Yosemite's Half Dome. She's currently at work on a collection of short stories.

N. AHERN is a freelance writer and editor specializing in travel, food, fitness, and parenting. She has written for magazines including *Elle, Men's Journal, Conde Nast Traveler, Health, American Way, Child, Yankee,* and *Fit Pregnancy*, and she has appeared on CNN, CNBC, and *Good Morning America*. She is currently at work on her first novel.

SARA BENINCASA is a comedian, writer, and talk show host on Sirius XM Satellite Radio. She's written for Nerve.com, The Onion News Network, the Travel Channel, and others. During the 2008 presidential campaign, she created original web video content for the humor site of *The Huffington Post,* 23/6 (www .236.com). Her Sarah Palin vlogs won the ECNY Award for Best Comedic Short Film and were shortlisted for the Webby Awards for Best Comedy Series and Best Individual Performance. She was also nominated for the ECNY Emerging Comic Award. She was a citizen journalist for the 2008 MTV Choose or Lose Street Team, part of MTV's Emmy Award-winning Think campaign. TV appearances include MTV's *Total Request Live* and CNN's *Situation Room with Wolf Blitzer.* (She was more psyched about the latter, as she fell in love with Wolf during his sensually arousing Gulf War coverage in '91, when his Cable ACE award-winning reportage stirred her ten-year-old loins to a spring awakening.) She is currently paying off a graduate degree in teaching from Columbia University by bringing her one-woman show, *Agorafabulous!*, to reasonably priced venues in a city near you. She's also writing a hilarious book about living with agoraphobia and panic attacks, also (tentatively) called *Agorafabulous!* Her website is www.sarabenincasa.com.

V. CALDER is a Massachusetts-based freelance writer who specializes in writing about health, nutrition, and mind/body issues. She has written for magazines such as *Men's Fitness, Fit Pregnancy, Parenting,* and *Walking,* where she was associate editor (and learned how to stride like a pro). As the mind/body editor of FitForAll.com, she not only realized the benefits of meditation, but she also got to work closely with Herbert Benson, MD, founder of the Mind/Body Medical Institute at Beth Israel Deaconess Hospital. In her free time, she likes to travel with her husband and two children. Next on her list: Italy's Amalfi Coast!

CELENA CIPRIASO is currently a writer's assistant at *All My Children* (yes, the soap with Erica Kane). She began her writing life as a poet and playwright before becoming a screenwriter. She pursued these goals at the dramatic writing program at NYU. She soon realized she sucked at writing fiction, so she decided to start writing nonfiction. Her theatre and spoken-word pieces have been performed in various places throughout New York City and along the East Coast. She has been published in the

HarperCollins anthology *Yell-Oh Girls! Emerging Voices Explore Culture, Identity, and Growing Up Asian American,* a Vassar literary magazine called *Asian Quilt,* AsianAvenue.com, and Rollick-Guides.com. She is currently working on her first memoir, and one of its chapters ("The What If Drink") was published in the online literary magazine *World Riot.* She'll always remember the last time she saw Lee, riding away in her car, the back of her Red Sox hat staring at her through the car's back window. And if she could talk to Lee now, she'd say, "The Red Sox aren't so bad. I'm even kinda a fan now."

JEAN COPELAND is a Connecticut-based writer and poet whose fiction has appeared in *Off the Rocks, Best Lesbian Love Stories 2009, Harrington Lesbian Literary Quarterly,* and *The First Line,* and on HotMetalPress.net and PrickoftheSpindle.com. After Barack Obama won the election, she and Val rekindled their friendship, avoiding politics like the high-school cheerleader they couldn't stand (and who now shops at their grocery store). Jean would like to express her gratitude to Governor Sarah Palin for getting her riled up enough to write this letter.

ANNA COX (www.ladyprofessor.com) is an assistant professor and director of the photography program at Longwood University, in Farmville, Virginia. Her writing has been published in *The Chronicle of Higher Education.* She and fellow contributor Jill Rothenberg are developing an anthology about women's relationships with their beds. Besides writing, Anna is an award-winning visual artist who exhibits her work nationally and internationally in cities such as New York, Toronto, Chicago,

Los Angeles, and Boston. She and Lara still drink bourbon and gingers and avoid Old Navy like the plague. Lara can finally zip her own pants.

SOPHIA DEMBLING lives in Dallas and is the author of *The Yankee Chick's Survival Guide to Texas*. Her work has been included in *Cat Women: Female Writers on Their Feline Friends* (Seal Press, 2007), *The Best Women's Travel Writing 2006*, and *The Best Women's Travel Writing 2009*. Sophia has had hundreds of articles and essays published in newspapers and magazines and on websites. She also blogs for the travel website World Hum, as well as on her own website, www.sophiadembling.com.

MARY EMERICK is a kayak ranger and wildland firefighter living in Sitka, Alaska. Most of her stories are written in a tent, either after a day on a fireline or while camping in the wilderness along southeast Alaska's remote coast. In previous lives, she has worked for the National Park Service and other agencies in Florida, Nevada, California, Idaho, and other states, as a wilderness ranger, tree planter, cave-tour guide, and panther-capture assistant. She grew up in northern Michigan and graduated from Michigan State University with a degree in creative writing, but meeting John's aunt, the woman she writes to in the letter, sidetracked her journalism-career ideas forever. She is still looking for John's aunt and hopes that she happens to pick up this book someday. Her articles and short stories have appeared in *The International Journal of Wilderness, Wildland Firefighter, Chicken Soup for the Nature Lover's Soul, Passages North,* and other publications. She is currently working on a memoir.

KARRIE GAVIN is a freelance writer who lives with her husband, Damian, and their dog, Dottie, in Philadelphia. She is the author of *Moon Philadelphia,* part of the esteemed Moon Handbooks guidebook series from Avalon Travel Publishing. Karrie has written for *USAirways* magazine, *AAA World, Philadelphia* magazine, *Pennsylvania Wine & Spirits,* and numerous wedding and shelter publications. She covers a wide variety of topics, but Philadelphia, travel, and relationships are her specialties. Karrie has a master's in journalism from Temple University, where she also taught public speaking. She is currently working on a memoir.

MICHELLE GOODMAN is author of *My So-Called Freelance Life: How to Survive and Thrive as a Creative Professional for Hire* and *The Anti 9-to-5 Guide: Practical Career Advice for Women Who Think Outside the Cube,* both published by Seal Press. Her writing has appeared in *The New York Times, Salon, Bust, Bitch, The Bark,* and *The Seattle Times;* on cnn.com and abcnews.com, and in several anthologies, including *Single State of the Union: Single Women Speak Out on Life, Love, and the Pursuit of Happiness* (Seal Press, 2007). She lives in Seattle with Buddy, her eighty-pound lapdog, and blogs about the freelance life at www.anti9to5guide.com.

JANE HODGES is a freelance writer in Seattle. Her fiction has appeared in *The Brooklyn Review,* and she has published essays in *Single State of the Union: Single Women Speak Out on Life, Love, and the Pursuit of Happiness* (Seal Press, 2007) and *The Seattle Weekly.* Her journalism has appeared in *The New York Times,* the *Wall Street Journal, Fortune, Business 2.0,* on msnbc.com and *The Seattle Times,* and many other print and online publications. She feels guilty every day about her unfinished novel and the loans she took out for an MFA in creative writing, and when she's not reading fiction or a day-old newspaper, she's reading friends' tarot cards. She's a loyal friend—but nobody puts Baby in a corner. Visit her at www.janehodges.net.

LORI HORVITZ's short stories, poetry, and personal essays have appeared in a variety of literary journals and anthologies, including *The Southeast Review, The Broome Review, The Salt River Review, Hotel Amerika, The Coe Review, Thirteenth Moon, The Mochila Review, Dos Passos Review,* and *Quarter After Eight.* She has been awarded writing fellowships from Fundación Valparaiso, Ragdale, Yaddo, Cottages at Hedgebrook, Virginia Center for the Creative Arts, and Blue Mountain Center. She is an associate professor of literature and language at the University of North Carolina at Asheville, where she teaches courses in creative writing, literature, and women's studies.

SUSAN JOHNSTON lives in Boston, where she works as a freelance writer by day and teaches writing and blogging by night. After sharing apartments with a few more roommates, she is pleased to report that she's moved into her very own shoebox studio. Susan's essays have appeared in *The Boston Globe, Chicken Soup for the Soul: Getting In . . . to College,* and *The Christian Science Monitor.* She also writes about career and lifestyle topics for Bankrate .com, DailyCandy.com, MediaBistro.com, *Self,* WritersWeekly .com, and many other places. Visit her website at www .susan-johnston.com or read about her writing adventures at www.urbanmusewriter.com.

ALICE LESCH KELLY is a freelance writer specializing in health and mind/body wellness. Her work has appeared in publications such as *More, Woman's Day, Shape, Fit Pregnancy, Viv, Triumph, The New York Times*, and the *Los Angeles Times*. She has coauthored four books, including *Be Happy Without Being Perfect*. She lives in Newton, Massachusetts, with her husband, Dave, and two sons, Steven and Scott. Her website is www.aliceleschkelly.com.

MARGARET LITTMAN is a freelance journalist who splits her time between Nashville and Chicago and wherever else her assignments take her. Her essays have appeared in the Seal Press anthologies *Woman's Best Friend: Women Writers on the Dogs in Their Lives* and *Cat Women: Female Writers on Their Feline Friends*, although she much prefers writing about other people's stories than her own. She is the author of *The Dog Lover's Companion to Chicago* and *VegOut Vegetarian Guide to Chicago* and is the editor of several other guidebooks. Her articles have been published in magazines ranging from *Wine Enthusiast* to *Art & Antiques*. She is at work on two book proposals, including *Dog-Friendly Life: A Guide for Those Who Want to Live With Their Dogs, Not For Their Dogs*. Read more of her work at www.littmanwrites.com.

DIMITY McDOWELL is a sports and fitness writer who started her magazine career in New York City, where she was on staff at *Women's Sports + Fitness, Self, ESPN The Magazine* and *Sports Illustrated Women*. During those six years, she covered a wide range of topics—everything from mainstream sports (hanging out in the Denver Broncos locker room was less fun than you'd think) to the extreme (jumping from an airplane was more fun than you'd think). A freelancer since 2000, she is a contributing editor for *Women's Health* and *Runner's World* magazines. She is also at work on her first book: an account of the intersection of running and mothering, cowritten with fellow contributor Sarah Bowen Shea. Dimity currently lives in Colorado Springs with her two kids, two dogs, and one husband.

JACQUELYN MITCHARD is the author of the number one *New York Times* bestselling novel *The Deep End of the Ocean,* which was chosen as the first book for Oprah Winfrey's Book Club and in 2007 named by *USA Today* as one of the most influential books of the past twenty-five years, second only to the Harry Potter series. She has subsequently written seven other bestselling novels—*The Most Wanted, A Theory of Relativity, Twelve Times Blessed, Christmas, Present, The Breakdown Lane, Cage of Stars,* and *Still Summer,* as well as an essay collection, *The Rest of Us: Dispatches from the Mothership.* The film version of *The Deep End of the Ocean*, starring Michelle Pfeiffer, was released in March 1999. *Still Summer* is currently in development for a Lifetime original film, and *Cage of Stars* is in development for an independent film by EMO Pictures. A former syndicated columnist for Tribune Media Services, Mitchard now is a contributing editor for *Parade* and *Wondertime* magazines, in addition to being a frequent contributor to magazines such as *Reader's Digest, Hallmark, More,* and *Real Simple.* Her screenplays include *A Serpent's Egg,* with Amy Paulsen, and *Doing Fine,* with John Roach. She is the founding organizer of One Writer's Place, a small residence for writers and artists healing through creativity after difficult life circumstances. Mitchard lives in Wisconsin with her husband, Christopher Brent, and their seven children. Her website is www.jackiemitchard.com.

CLAIRE MURPHY is the pseudonym of a writer who lives in the West. Her work has appeared in a variety of publications, including *The New York Times* and *O*.

JILL ROTHENBERG and her e-mail recipient, Melissa Trainer, are both Colorado transplants who fell in love with Boulder in their Grateful Dead days more than twenty years ago, when they were most definitely not the fashionistas who are making waves through town today. Instead, they wore hemp necklaces and clogs from El Loro on Pearl Street and shapeless gauze skirts from the racks outside of Boulder Army Navy. These days, you'll find them training for long-distance races all over the state—Jill as a trail runner and dirt biker and Melissa as a former professional downhill mountain bike racer and competitive skier. They still hang out at the Boulder Whole Foods and dress up for their nights out at the St. Julien (where patrons actually wear something other than Crocs) or when they venture into the big city of Denver, where Jill lives—across the street from REI, of course. Jill works as a managing editor at the Geological Society of America and an online instructor for mediabistro.com. Her work has appeared in the *San Francisco Chronicle, Urban Moto Magazine,* and *Woman's Best Friend: Women Writers on the Dogs in Their Lives* (Seal Press, 2006).

JOSHUNDA SANDERS is a writer, journalist, and aspiring librarian. Her writing and reporting has appeared in *Bitch, Vibe,* and *Suede* magazines and in the *Houston Chronicle,* the *San Francisco Chronicle*, the *Seattle Post-Intelligencer*, and *The Dallas Morning News*. Her essays have appeared in *Secrets and Confidences: The Complicated*

Truth about Women's Friendships (Seal Press, 2004) and *Homelands: Women's Journeys Across Race, Place, and Time* (Seal Press, 2006). Her poems have been published in *Quiet Storm: Voices of Young Black Poets* and *Dialogue* magazine.

JEN KARUZA SCHILE has written profiles, features, and personal essays for both trade and mainstream publications. She's been a regular writer and correspondent for *National Fisherman* magazine and was also published in *Pacific Fishing*. Her personal essays were included in the anthologies *A Matter of Choice: 25 People Who Transformed Their Lives* and *Steady as She Goes: Women's Adventures at Sea*. Jen facilitates a writing circle for the Story Circle Network, a national organization of women writers, and received an honorable mention in the memoir category of the Writer's Digest Writing Competition. Jen can be reached at www.jen karuzaschile.com or on her blog, Highliners and Homecomings, which celebrates the life of commercial-fishing families. She lives in Bellingham, Washington.

DENISE SCHIPANI became a writer in part because of Karen, the friend she wrote to for this book. A former editor for such magazines as *Bridal Guide, American Baby, Child, All Woman*, and *Zest* in the U.K., Denise is now a freelance writer and editor. She's written features, columns, and essays for *American Baby, Parents, Parenting, Parent & Child, Redbook, Real Simple, Family Circle, Woman's Day, Women's Health*, and *The Washington Post*, among others. She and her husband, Robert, are raising two sons, Daniel and James, in Huntington, New York. Read more of her work at www.deniseschipani.com.

JENNA SCHNUER has a tendency to swerve between very social and "I just want to be alone" moods, but the NYC-based freelance writer is wildly loyal to her friends (though admittedly, not so good at keeping in touch at times). When she's not thinking deep thoughts about friendship (so, that would be most of the time), Jenna spends her days writing about travel, food, and random bits of this and that. Her magazine credits include *American Way, Continental, National Geographic Traveler*, and many others. Along with fellow contributor Sophia Dembling, Jenna cowrites the Flyover America blog on World Hum (www.worldhum.com). Want more? Visit her online at www.jennaschnuer.com.

SARAH BOWEN SHEA is a freelance writer who specializes in writing about fitness, health, gear, and parenting. She writes for a variety of magazines, including *Runner's World, Self, Health,* and *Fit Pregnancy*, and she is the athletic footwear editor for *Shape*. Sarah's especially proud of the pieces she's written for the Thursday *Styles* section of *The New York Times*. She lives with her husband and three young children, including boy–girl twin preschoolers. Showing off her nurturing side, Sarah had her first book published in February: *The Essential Breastfeeding Log: A Feedings Tracker and Baby-Care Organizer for Nursing Moms* (see www.essentialbreast feedinglog.com). Sarah has run five marathons and is a competitive Masters rower. Ever a braggart, Sarah blogs about juggling parenting, work, and working out at marathonmoms.blog spot.com. Her next book—tentatively titled *Run Like a Mother* and coauthored with fellow contributor Dimity McDowell—is due out in spring 2010.

ROBIN SILBERGLEID is assistant professor of English at Michigan State University, where she teaches literature and creative writing. She is the author of the chapbook *Pas de Deux: Prose and Other Poems* (Basilisk Press, 2006), and her poems and essays have appeared in journals including *The Truth about the Fact, River Oak Review, Crab Orchard Review*, and the *Cream City Review*, for which she was nominated for a Pushcart Prize. Her collection of poems *The Baby Book* began as a piece she wrote for J.'s son on the occasion of his birth, a poem that never actually made it into the collection. He is, however, included in *Texas Girl,* a book-length memoir that deals with becoming a single mother by choice. Robin is looking for publishers for both books. Following the birth of her daughter, Robin moved to Michigan; she has many friends in East Lansing, but they are not J.

MAGGIE LAMOND SIMONE is an award-winning columnist and author. Her humor and observational essays have appeared for six years in *Family Times,* an award-winning monthly parenting magazine in Syracuse, New York, and *The Advertiser,* a weekly newspaper in East Aurora, New York. Her essays have appeared in *Cosmopolitan,* and are included in *Chicken Soup for the Soul: My Resolution, Chicken Soup for the New Mom's Soul, Chicken Soup for the Soul in Menopause, Misadventures of Moms and Disasters of Dads,* and *Hello, Goodbye.* Her first children's picture book, *Sophie's Sounds,* was released in May 2007, and she is awaiting the release of two more picture books, *Losing Decker* and *Timmy and the Timepiece.* She's won multiple awards through Parenting Publications of America. She is a member of the Society of Children's Book Writers and Illustrators and the New York Press Association, and she is also an adjunct instructor of English at Bryant & Stratton College, in Clay, New York. She earned a bachelor's degree from Hobart and William Smith colleges and a master's degree from the S. I. Newhouse School of Communications, at Syracuse University. Simone lives in central New York with her husband and two children.

GABRIELLE STUDENMUND has written for *Self, Shape, Fitness,* and *Glamour* magazines. She is a former fitness editor at *Self* and was an editor at SportsforWomen.com and *American Health* magazine. After a serious bike accident in 2002, she now earns disability and lives in Southern Pines, North Carolina, with her cat, Lucy. She has recently started writing again for a local publication, *Pinestraw* magazine. She hopes to get more freelance magazine assignments and plans to one day write a memoir about becoming disabled and her journey to recovery. Gabrielle graduated with honors from the University of Wyoming in 1998, with a degree in journalism and a minor in women's studies.

SHANNON HYLAND-TASSAVA is a writer, clinical psychologist, and mother to two young daughters. Having left her private psychotherapy practice and a hectic urban lifestyle shortly before the birth of her second child, she currently focuses on freelance writing, consulting, and at-home parenting in a small rural college town in southern Minnesota. She has written for *Motherwords* magazine, The Mothers Movement Online, *Macalester Today* magazine, WorkItMom.com, *Girlfriends* magazine, and MotherVerse online. She writes an occasional mind/body health column for her town's newspaper and is a health and wellness consultant for clinics and

businesses. She writes daily about her adventures in modern motherhood at www.mamainwonderland.blogspot.com.

JUDY SUTTON TAYLOR lives with her family in Chicago, where
she's the kids editor at *Time Out Chicago*. She also writes about
food and fitness. Her work has appeared in the *Chicago Tribune,
Cooking Light, Self, Good Housekeeping,* and *Chicago* magazine. Her
semester abroad, way back when, gave her a permanent itch to
travel, and she's been lucky enough to mix work with pleasure
by contributing to guidebooks for *Fodor's, Mobil, Gault Millau,* and
Little Black Book. Her essay "Twenty Years Later" is for Michele,
who always joked that her parents could only afford one "l" and
whom she talks with often . . . and always on December 21.

TRACY TEARE is a freelance writer hailing from the Maine coast,
near the city of Portland. Writing about friendship was a wel-
come change up from her usual fare: mainly fitness and parenting, with some health and travel for good measure. Tracy's
work has been published in a number of magazines, such as
Real Simple, Health, Prevention, Fit Pregnancy, Wondertime, and
Family Fun. She is also a regular contributor to Disney's family.
com, where (much to her girls' dismay) she records many of her
parenting adventures, as well as tips on favorite New England
destinations. Tracy has also written extensively about walking
and has contributed to two books—*Walking through Pregnancy*
and *Pedometer Walking*—with walking guru Mark Fenton. Tracy also contributed essays to Seal Press's *Woman's Best Friend:
Women Writers on the Dogs in Their Lives* and *Cat Women: Female
Writers on Their Feline Friends.* Though Tracy's family of three

daughters keeps her hopping, she vows not to let so many years roll by before she sees her buddies from high school (especially Amy) again.

ROBIN TROY is a professor of fiction writing and director of the MFA program in creative writing at Southern Connecticut State University. She is the author of the novel *Floating*, as well as a forthcoming novel, *Liberty Lanes*. She received her MFA from the University of Montana in Missoula, where she was also a staff writer for the *Missoula Independent* newspaper. She lives in New Haven, Connecticut, with her husband, daughter, pound dog, and two turtles—and only wishes there were fewer miles between her and her spectacular friend Evaun so that she would never again miss another co-birthday celebration, afternoon at Harold's, drive to Browns Lake, or wing-dingy with the whole gang (the Wild Ones) at the bowling alley.

BEVIN WALLACE spent much of her twenties getting over the fact that she never made it big-time as a performer (although her best friend and subject of her letter did once dance on stage with The Tubes). Between stints as a book publicist, bookseller, nonprofit-event coordinator, and PR gal in cities like New York, San Francisco, and Denver, she rediscovered her love of outdoor adventure. Some of her adult escapades include trekking in Nepal and Peru, backcountry skiing in Europe with her two tiny kids ("les petites Alpinistes"), climbing about half of Colorado's 14ers, cycling in France, and completing the California AIDS ride from San Francisco to L.A. As a former editor at *Skiing* magazine, she's traveled and skied all over the world—including Japan, Austria,

Utah, Switzerland, Quebec, and Las Vegas. She left *Skiing* in 2003 to give her knees a rest and to serve as editor-in-chief of *Warren Miller's SnoWorld*. Today she works as a copywriter and continues to write for *Skiing, Ski, National Geographic Adventure, Delicious Living, Elevation Outdoors*, and other publications. She lives in Denver with her husband, David; her seven-year-old son, Sean, and her four-year-old daughter, Lauren—all of them are avid skiers, and they just love to look at photos of mom decked out for The Clash concert in 1983.

KRISTINA WRIGHT (www.kristinawright.com) has been calling herself a writer since Miss Gilmore gave her an A+ on her first short story in the first grade. In the thirty-five years since, she has traded in her wide-rule paper and fat pencils for a Power-Book laptop, and she has managed to rack up hundreds of writing credits for everything from greeting cards to book reviews. Her first novel was published in 1999, and her short fiction has appeared in more than seventy anthologies. She holds a bachelor's in English and a master's in humanities (with an emphasis on women's studies and popular culture) and teaches both English and humanities at her local community college. She lives in Virginia with her husband, Jay, and a menagerie of pets. Her friend and penpal Julia died in February 2009, thirteen months after her stroke. She would have been ninety in November. Her memory—and her words—live on.

acknowledgments

The best thing about them thar anthology thingamajigs is that I don't have to toil away by myself. Sure, I'm technically in my home office, typing away solo, but you know what I mean: It's an anthology, after all, which means everyone comes together (group hug everybody—you in the back, get in here, don't be shy!).

This is my third anthology, and luckily I have strong-armed a few writers into coming along for yet another ride. First of all, to my great (and hysterical) pals Robin Troy and Dimity McDowell, who continually amaze me with their word-wizardly ways and their supercool personalities. A high five to repeat offenders from previous anthologies: Jenna Schnuer (thanks for the Hallmark moment while editing your letter, my friend, ha ha!), Katie Arnold, Judy Sutton Taylor, Margaret Littman, Sophia Dembling, and Tracy Teare. To fellow Portland writing buddy Sarah Bowen Shea, a hearty shout-out, not only for contributing, but also for showing off your "connector" skills by putting me in touch with so many fabulous wordsmiths. To contributors I'd never worked with before but knew (or knew of)—Jane Hodges, Michelle Goodman, Alice Lesch Kelly, Bevin Wallace, Denise Schipani, Susan Johnston, N. Ahern, V. Calder, and Claire Murphy—it was a blast to work with you all. To Jacquelyn Mitchard for penning a story that makes me cry (okay, sob openly) every time I read it, a deep bow for your contribution. Finally, a heartfelt "thank you" to my friend Gabrielle Studenmund for bravely sharing her touching story and for not minding my many nosy (and probably pesky) questions.

You thought that was mushy? We haven't even gotten started, people! (Rolling up sleeves. . . .)

I've had the great fortune of having the best friend a girl would ever want, right out of life's starting gates: my mom, Penny. My mom has taught me how to be an empathetic listener, a gentle advice-giver, and a strong yet soft presence. She also taught me how to shriek with laughter often and weep openly just as often. It's not a mystery why many friends turn to me for a sounding board. After all, I've always had her as mine, so I've learned from a pro.

Of course, it's not just the two McMorris girls here—my sister, Erin, is always the one I can turn to for sharing those hysterical "Oh my god I can't believe that just happened to me" moments and the "Gawd, I'm so annoyed and need to vent" stories, and she's always an empathetic voice on the other end of the line. Erin's also the one who will tell you how you really look in those pants (or will be the first to notice that your eyebrows look fabulous), and girls, you know how important that is! Even though she tells me I can never talk about her in my blog or in an essay, I'm ignoring her in this instance. So there—neener neener!

I'm a person who believes that when it comes to friends, it takes a village—a cornucopia of different personalities, if you will. To Anne Marie Moss, for always making me laugh; to Jacki Herb, for being that "wise" sounding board to whom I feel I could tell anything (and whose laugh makes me laugh); and to my new friend Michelle Banks, who delighted me earlier this year by moving from Ohio to Portland and making this girl realize that, yes, insta-friendships can still be had (and who makes me laugh with her zippy one-liners). Of course, always, to my McBuddies, who spoiled me early on with true friendships: Andy (whom I met in kindergarten and was my inseparable "twin" straight through to high school and beyond), Diane (whom I kinda met in kindergarten, on the bus; see page 227), and Heather, who didn't have the grand fortune to go to Kenwood Elementary (ha!) but whom we befriended later on at Bowling Green High School—I always know I can turn to her in a rough moment . . . or for planning another hysterical McTrip!

But the world doesn't live on girls alone. So a hug to my boyfriend, Eric Hedaa, for his endless patience as I toiled, for always listening to funny sentences and moving phrases as I worked on the book, and for encouraging me every word of the way. Cheers to good pal Pete-osky Posey for always guffawing at my manic editing stories and for his offers of home-delivered whiskey when I mentioned I had a once-in-a-blue-moon hankering for the stuff while reading an essay that prominently featured bourbon. And a "Yo!" to my long-lost (and, through Facebook, found alive and well in Portland) Indiana U. buddy, Josh Alsberg, who was the genius behind the lens of my About the Editor photo and who expertly managed to only feature one of my chins without resorting to Photoshop. You're a pro. (Check out his website at www.joshalsbergimages.com) And to my knights in shining armor at the Apple store in Bridgeport Village (Can I get a "Whoop! Whoop!"?) for helping a girl in several computer crises, for swooping in with Kleenex to dry my tears, for offering to waive fees, and for working super-fast to make sure my book wasn't (gulp) lost in a computer crash. They say once you go Mac you never go back, and now I know why.

Last, but certainly not least, this book would never exist without the never-ending faith (even when I don't deserve such faith) of my cool-as-a-cuke editor Krista Lyons and the wonderful publishing house that is Seal Press. And even though she's no longer an editor at Seal, a secret hand-clasp and rock-on-sista fist pump into the air for Jill Rothenberg, who originally came up with the idea that would be my first anthology and who graciously brought me along for the ride. Hey, lady? You rule.

P.S. Thanks also to my fuzzy coworkers, Luey and Lily, and to Twizzlers, Pepsi Max, and my favorite bartender, Kim, at MashTun brewpub (where I'd carry my laptop during late deadline nights), without whom I woulda been lost.